Relentless Determination

Harnessing The Will To Win, To Survive, To Overcome

Andre R. Thornton

A.R. Thornton Publications

Copyright © 2020 Andre R. Thornton

All rights reserved. No part of this publication may be reproduced, distributed, or transmitted in any form or by any means, including photocopying, recording, or other electronic or mechanical methods, without the prior written permission of the publisher.

All rights reserved.

ISBN: 978-0-578-69629-4

DEDICATION

"The race is not given to the swift but nor the battle to the strong"

This book is dedicated to those who have helped shape my life; good, bad or indifferent you were an integral part of who I am.

I miss you, I love you and I thank you. -Dre

Wilbert E. Wright

Lillian Corrine Thornton

Ronald J. Thornton (Unc)

CONTENTS

	Introduction	i
1	Caution Rough Road Ahead	1
2	What Is Determination Anyway	9
3	Decide and Stand By It	16
4	How To Build Determination	24
5	Remember Your Why	36
6	Never Look Back	50
7	Focus on What You Do Now	56
8	What Are You Willing To Sacrifice	61
9	Let Your Measurement of Success Drive You Forward	65
10	Call The Shots	79

INTRODUCTION

What if I told you that success isn't what you think it is?

That's right. A lot of people are under the impression that success is usually reserved for the smartest, most beautiful, and most talented people. Well, the truth is that's often the opposite.

If you look at people who are at the top of their game or industry, the ones who prevail aren't necessarily the ones with the highest IQ. It's quite shocking to find out that frequently, they are not the best-looking people.

Of course, they're also not the ugliest, but they're usually in the middle when it comes to the looks department. When it comes to talent, a lot are in the middle of the curve.

How come? It turns out that successful people are the ones who manage to overcome one challenge after another. They frequently get hit with one setback after another, and they were able to stick with their plan long enough for them to prevail. Similarly, successful individuals tend to outlast competitors and stick around long enough until almost everybody has dropped out.

Finally, those who make it to the top often can put in the effort into their journey until their journey somehow changes them. It is this change that "qualified" these people for victory.

What do you do until you reach that point of victory? This is the question that you have to ask yourself if you want to make it all the way. If you want to achieve the kind of success that you know you're capable of producing, you have to wrap your head around this question.

Usually, people don't ask this question. They really don't. Instead, they fill their heads with technicalities. Who do I need to know? What are the things that I need to do? What are the specifics of the tasks that are going to be assigned to me or the projects that I need to assume?

As important as these questions may be, when it comes to achieving ultimate success, they're not as important as the questions you need to be asking. In addition to the issue I mentioned above, you should also ask yourself another question.

You should ask yourself, how do you hang on when success is not assured? How do you find the energy to keep going forward and doing your best even when success doesn't even appear that it will happen anytime soon?

These are the hard questions that so many of us tend to overlook. It is no surprise that the vast majority of people who go after the same prize—whether it's academic, financial, physical, or romantic, don't get to where we want to go.

The truth? Success is mostly attitude. Aptitude will come later.

I know this comes as a shock to a lot of people. I know it came as a shock to me. For the longest time, I was trained to believe that I just need to cross my T's and dot my I's, know the right people, know the structure, do what I need to do, know what I need to know, and eventually, success will come. Unfortunately, that's not enough. Why?

If you want to be successful in life, you will need the right attitude for the rough road ahead. Believe me. It is going to be hard. There's going to be discouragement and unforeseen challenges. It's as if you laid out this perfect map for you to get from point A to point B. Everything seems like it's going as planned.

Before you know it, something hits you from left field, and you find yourself back on square one. What do you do in that situation?

How do you find the will to do things all over again and still keep pushing forward? How would you react if something else happens after you've made some progress, and you find yourself back on square one?

CAUTION ROUGH ROAD AHEAD

The road ahead may be filled with opposition. This may be one person or a group of people who seem to have something against you. Whatever this specific reason may be, they try to block every step you make. What do you do? This goes on day after day, week after week, month after month, and yes—year after year.

Similarly, even if you're making some progress, you can't help but think to yourself, am I doing the right thing? Is this all worth it? What would happen if I get to my destination? These and many other doubts fill your head.

Before you know it, each step forward becomes even more unsteady. You start to doubt yourself. You begin to question your decisions. You find yourself second-guessing the significant decisions you are making now and the choices that you have to make in the future. What happens then?

It could also be that this whole project you have set up for yourself just seems like it's going to take forever. You know that you're going to be waiting.

For example, if you're going to be climbing up that corporate ladder, at some point, you're going to have to wait for somebody to either get fired or die. What do you do? Do you jump ship? Do you change horses in the middle of crossing a stream?

Finally, even if you can meet with some success, you might not like the person that you have become. When you look at yourself in the mirror, it might dawn on you that you have changed in a way that you're not exactly comfortable with. It turns out that the goal that you have set for yourself requires that you have to become a different person.

To get what you want, you're going to have to change. And I'm not talking about a change of hairstyle here and there or change in fashion taste. I'm talking about fundamental, profound, and personal changes like overcoming fear, setting aside your pride, and becoming a more resourceful person when throughout all this time, you thought that you're utterly dependent on others.

Are you willing to make that change? Do you have it in you to make that kind of sacrifice to become the person that would achieve the success that you desire?

In all the scenarios that I have described above, one thing is clear. You have to find the will to keep going. The bottom line? You have to overcome two things.

First, you have to overcome your external challenges. These are people and situations beyond your control. For whatever reason, things just stacked up in such a way that you are going to be facing one set of opposition and one obstacle after another.

Are you up for the job? Even if you've knocked out the first few hurdles, do you have it in you to go all the way? Because this is not going to let up. It's not like these people, or these situations are going to go away anytime soon.

Similarly, are you willing to overcome your second challenge? I'm talking about your internal doubts. This is that part of you that tells you: you are not worth it, you're not good enough, you're not smart, you're not resourceful, you're not good-looking enough, people don't like you, you don't belong here, you don't deserve that goal—I can go on and on.

All of these ideas in the back of your mind take many different forms. However, it can be reduced to internal doubts, insecurities, low self-esteem, and self-confidence issues.

Let's get one thing clear. Even if you bolt out of that gate at the beginning of the race with all the power, poise, and potential you could muster, eventually, these internal challenges have a way of slowing you down. It's like you're trying to run a 500-meter race with running shoes made out of cement.

The worst part? You tied them on yourself. It's not like somebody pointed a gun at your head and said, "I want you to doubt yourself and question your capabilities." You did it to yourself.

Can you find the will to keep going even in the face of these internal and external challenges? This is where your mindset comes in.

If you were to look at the people who make it and those that don't, the difference is not aptitude. That long trail of people who have given up or who have settled may be more talented than you. You best believe that a lot of them are smarter than you. Many of them are quite attractive.

They may even be more physically appealing than you. Yet there they are—broken and fallen. They have given up. And here you are at the crossroads, where it's lonely. When you look ahead and you see the successful people, they're not any different from you.

They're not the most attractive or the most intelligent. But there they are at the pinnacle of success. They are at the top of their game. What is the difference?

Well, it's not outside of you. It's all in your head. This is called the power of mindset. How does mindset affect your daily waking life?

You probably have heard of a positive mental attitude or how a positive or a sunny disposition can make things turn out for the better. You have probably heard this many times.

Just like with most people, you probably doubt it as well. I really can't say I blame you because it does seem like some BS. I get all that. But here's how it works. You see, the signals that the world sends your way, it is you who give these signals meaning. By signal, I'm talking about the things that you can see, hear, taste, touch, and smell. These are the data points that your five senses pick up. All these pass through your mindset.

Your mindset then interprets these and creates thoughts. Do you think thoughts just float out of you with absolutely no effect? No. They have a significant impact.

Your thoughts, or how you frame and interpret things, create an emotional state. They are never emotionally neutral.

What do you think happens when you are in a particular emotional state? Chances are you will say something, or do something stupid based on those emotions. This is where things get interesting. When you take action—it can be as simple as saying something at a specific point in time to somebody, it would have consequences.

Do you think these consequences just flow off your back like water rolling off a duck's back? Of course not. The process repeats itself because these consequences form the external stimuli, which then gets filtered by your mindset. You think a certain way, and then you're in an emotional state. Then you take specific actions or say certain things. The process produces consequences. Again and again, it goes.

Until and unless you fully understand how this works out, you will continue to struggle. You'll look at your life as this massive movie screen that seems to show scene after scene out of your life. But there's something strange going on.

You can see all the scenes and they look so familiar, but there's nothing you can do to change the story. All you can do is just to sit back and passively watch your life unfold in front of you.

You can't direct the plot. You don't have a voice over the action. It's as if your life was pre-scripted ahead of time for your viewing. I wish I could say that you were enjoying all of this. But that sense of powerlessness sinks to your very bones. It's as if you're watching a train wreck, and there's nothing you can do. Is that what you want for yourself? Of course, not.

RELENTLESS DETERMINATION

Most people wouldn't want this for themselves. Unfortunately, this is the kind of life too many of us live. We feel that there's nothing we can change because once that external stimulus hits, it's as if our mindset just kicks into action.

Everything that we say and do, they are foregone conclusions. We're in this emotional state, and all these things just flow out of it. Then we live out a certain kind of life.

However, I want you to understand that while it may be tough to change your actions because they're habitual and while it may almost seem impossible to change your emotional triggers and reactions, you can still change these series of events. How? You can change your mindset.

You might not be able to change the data points or external stimuli that the world sends your way. You may not have much control over the things that you see, hear, touch, taste, and smell. Yet, you can always choose how you respond. This is always the ultimate choice.

The good news is you can decide to make that choice today. You're not trapped in mindlessly repeating the same pattern before. For example, if the mental image of an ex-friend who stabbed you in the back and stole money from you flashes in your mind, you don't necessarily have to freak out. You don't necessarily have to feel angry, betrayed and bitter.

If that image of that boss that you had during your first corporate job who said certain things in front of a lot of people during a meeting with you present comes to mind, you don't have to feel humiliated. You don't have to start thinking that all people in authority have it against you or that there's something wrong with you. These are your choices.

You could always choose your mindset. If you choose your mindset, you would be able to choose your interpretation of the stimuli the world sends your way.

If you can understand this, then you will be able to create a positive feedback loop. There are always at least two ways to interpret a set of stimuli.

For example, going back to the case of that first boss. It could be that the boss was just making a joke and he had a particular style. You're not doing yourself any favors interpreting that joke, which he repeats in his way with many other co-workers of yours as something distinctly against you.

Just because you felt embarrassed, it doesn't necessarily mean that it was all about you. That could be the person's style of breaking the ice, or that's just a quirk of his personality.

The question is, what are you going to do about it? Are you going to keep carrying that memory of what you interpreted as personal humiliation on your shoulders for the rest of your professional life? Are you going to let it poison your career because now you have an unhealthy view of people in authority?

Or are you going to select a different interpretation? This requires a different mindset. The different interpretation, of course, is that that's just who he is. He likes to crack jokes that may come off as insults or at the expense of other people.

By interpreting that memory differently, you can create a positive feedback loop. He was comfortable enough with you to crack that joke about your performance and not necessarily about you. This means that he was able to trust you because if you are fragile, he probably wouldn't want to do that. He wouldn't want to undermine his organization.

At the end of the day, you and the rest of the staff are the people responsible for bringing food to the corporate table. It would be foolish of him to insult, embarrass, or otherwise dehumanize his team. It would be like he's shooting himself in the foot.

So, when you look at that memory again from a different perspective, your part of the team. You're part of the people he trusts. What kind of feedback loop do you think this would create?

Well, you would feel like you belong. Just like somebody who belongs, you are more likely to take other actions to please your coworkers and teammates.

Guess what happens? They will tell inside jokes again that indicates that you are one of them. So, you feel even more connected. You feel even more dedicated to the common cause or goal of the organization, so you do your best again, and again, and again. This feedback loop keeps getting better and better because your results improve, and you feel more bonded to the organization.

By extension, you feel more worthy. You start taking more pride in your work. Before you know it, you begin to realize that you are super competent. You're part of the team. People are trusting you.

Isn't this a much better interpretation? Does this mindset lead not only to better emotions but to better results? Compare this with what you were doing before.

That joke that is in the fuzzy, murky recesses of your memory, only has one interpretation, as far as you're concerned. It's an embarrassment. It's as if your boss put you in the middle of the presentation as you go through your PowerPoint, and strip down your clothes. Everybody laughed and pointed their fingers.

If that's how you interpret that joke, then it's no surprise that every time you find yourself being asked to give a presentation or to take the lead, it's like the death of you. You will do a million and one things just to get away from that kind of assignment. The more you push off doing tasks that challenge your public presentation and project leadership skills, you become more and more ineffective.

Please understand that competence, confidence, and self-esteem go hand in hand when it comes to mindset. If you pick the wrong mindset, all these are negatively affected, and you go on a downward spiral. You end up grinding yourself down.

There's nobody else doing it to you. It's not like your boss is towering over your shoulders, pointing a gun at your head, and commanding you to be miserable and ineffective. You're doing it to yourself.

Mindset is crucial to success

Not only do you have to adopt the right mindset to interpret external stimuli in such a way that you will be able to succeed. You also need the right mindset to develop relentless determination.

The secret to relentless determination is to create in your head a self-reinforcing motivation system. That's the first step. It must begin in your mindset.

Once you adopt the right mindset, you start taking actions that reinforce your motivation. This is how you become relentlessly determined. It wouldn't matter what opposition you face, nor would it matter what kind of unforeseen circumstances hit you from left field.

Whether it involves forces of nature, virus epidemics, the death of somebody powerful, or other unforeseen circumstances, you will find yourself pushing forward. Nobody will be able to rob you of the motivation to put one foot in front of the other no matter how difficult and no matter how seemingly insurmountable the obstacles in front of you. This is the secret I will teach you in this book.

How do you create a self-reinforcing motivation system that starts internally, but projects out to your real world? See you in the next section.

WHAT IS DETERMINATION ANYWAY

Determination can be defined as finding the drive that you need to consistently do things that you need to do to produce a specific outcome. Put simply, if your car is your efforts and your destination is your goal, determination is the amount of gas, the battery charge, and other things propelling your car.

All these amounts to the power you need to get to where you need to go. So far, so good? This is where a lot of people get determination wrong. They get confused. Before they know it, they start to stumble.

If anything, determination is clear. It's not fuzzy. You set your sight on a goal and the goal is clear to you. It's well defined and you spelled it out in writing. Your efforts at getting to your goal are conscious. It's not like you just set up a goal for yourself all clear and specific, but somehow, someway, you find yourself achieving that goal.

It doesn't work that way. Your steps towards that goal are conscious. You don't luck into it. it doesn't fall on you. Things don't magically "fall into place". Your striving for that goal is conscious. You're driven towards that clear goal just as what you're doing is also clear to you.

With all this said, determination can be traced to a specific point in time. You can't say to yourself "It just happened. I woke up one day and all my dreams were realized." Usually, success doesn't work this way.

To be determined, a lot of things have to happen. It is no this fuzzy collection of tendencies, gut feel, intuition, and plain old luck. It doesn't work that way.

Determination starts with a decision

RELENTLESS DETERMINATION

So, how do you get the drive to constantly do what you need to do to get to where you need to go? Where do you get this inward power to overcome the obstacles, setbacks, and delays that are bound to happen?

It first starts with a decision. I know you're probably rolling your eyes. You're probably thinking "I make decisions all day and a lot of them don't really lead to something big." When it comes to determination, we're talking about a different kind of decision.

First, you select a goal and then you decide to go for it. Again, it's very easy to be dismissive at this definition. After all, don't we make decisions and set up goals for the future? Here's the problem. Just because you have a goal and it seems so crystal clear in your mind, just visualizing or thinking you have conceptualized such a goal is never the same as deciding to go for it.

In other words, you can trace your decision at a specific point in time. You can say to yourself "At a certain date or period in my life, I decided to pursue this goal instead of something else." In other words, deciding to go for your goal is different from just being clear about what to do.

Let's get one thing out of the way. You can have all sorts of plans and they may seem to make a lot of sense to you. You could've even written them down in logical order. Everything seems to fall into place on paper.

But this is all intellectual realization. Just because you're clear about what you need to do and the sequence of actions you need to take doesn't mean that you have decided. What you're doing is you're just getting in the car.

You've selected a specific car and you have selected a destination. So far, so good. But what is missing? You have to decide to take action. It has a starting point. You have to put in the key into the ignition and turn it. The engine has to turn over and the car has to go forward.

Determination is also different from plain action

When you have determined a goal and decided to go for it, this is different from just plain action. A lot of people just take action for the sake of doing something

People do this all the time. In reality, they're actually not doing what they need to do to achieve their goals. Why? They compartmentalize their actions. They know that up ahead, they have to take a different direction when the time comes.

As different conditions appear, they have to bend. Maybe they even have to take a detour. This means you have to be quick on your toes. You have to accept the fact that as you work towards your goal, things can change on an almost day to day basis.

For a lot of people, this is too much of a commitment. So they'd rather break it all down to just taking an action that they already know. They're already familiar with a certain type of action, so they just content themselves to doing that one day after the next.

The problem is they're not being versatile nor flexible. It's no surprise that a lot of people find themselves running in place. Don't get me wrong, they put in the effort. They break out in a sweat, they pay money to invest in whatever it is they're doing, they're taking action. No doubt about that.

But there they are, stuck in place. You know you're determined when you make a decision and you give it all you've got. This means you don't coast. You don't stick to what is comfortable or convenient.

You take risks. You look at new possibilities and uncover opportunities on the way forward. It may well turn out that the goal that you had originally set may be small potatoes. Maybe you should set your sights on something higher, more valuable, and bigger.

This, of course, means it's going to be more challenging. Are you up for it? This is different from just taking action. This means risk-taking and pushing the envelope. That's the kind of decision that determination requires.

Determination is different from just emotional clarity

Please understand that it's very easy to get pumped up about a goal. I'm sure the last time you daydreamed, you were really excited. Who wouldn't want to live in a multi-million-dollar mansion? What's not to love about rolling in town in a Ferrari?

It's easy to understand all of these from an emotional perspective. It comes in a flash. It seems so vivid. You can't wait to get started. In fact, a lot of people, when they set up their goals, they can't help but use a very common word: passion.

They say to themselves and anybody else willing to listen that they are passionate about their goal. So far, so good. But here comes the hard part. Passion eventually runs out. Just like a car running out of gas, eventually, you will find yourself running on the fumes of passion. What do you do then?

This is why it's really important to understand that the decision that you are going to make as you go for your goal with everything you have involves a long term commitment. Put simply, this commitment to do what you need to do day after day, week after week, month after month, and if need be, year after year goes beyond infatuation or bright flashes of motivation.

We're talking commitment. This is crucial for determination. Why? On certain days, you're probably going to hop out of the bed. You're bright-eyed, bushy-tailed, and you're ready to kick butt and take names. That's how pumped up you are.

You have so much energy to accomplish your objectives for that day because you know that if you knock them out, you'll get closer and closer to your big goals. Sounds awesome, right?

Unfortunately, those days are few and far between. Once you realize that trying to achieve your goals actually takes work and it's shaping up to be more of a marathon instead of a sprint, your view changes. You can't help it. nobody can blame you.

It turns out that this is going to be a long haul, long-distance trip. You have to remain emotionally engaged during those days. On certain days, you don't even want to get out of bed. You feel tired, even defeated.

At the back of your mind, you're thinking "I've put in all this time. I've broken my back for this dream of mine. But the road ahead seems so long. Where does it end? Is it even worth it? What am I doing with my life? Why does everybody else around me seem more successful or happy?"

You're going to have to weather those days. Those days are going to come fast and furious. As I mentioned earlier, those days are going to be more common than the days you wake up excited, passionate, and pumped up.

Determination starts with a decision to continue to pursue your goal even when the emotional engagement is not there. It is a matter of commitment. Even if it doesn't feel good, you're still going to have to do it.

Even if it feels like you have lost all passion, you're still going to have to go through with it not just today, or the day after, and the day after that. This decision point is not to be taken lightly. This decision point where you mentally isolate that point in time to go for your dreams involves an intricate dance between your body and your mind.

Determination intertwines your mind and body

When you consciously and clearly say to yourself or even to somebody with you that you have decided to pursue a specific goal, you are triggering a chain reaction that can help you tap the determination you need to achieve that goal.

For this to happen, you have to be clear about the fact that this can happen. How? You have to intend every word you say as you make your decision. When you do that, the words coming out of your mouth are just an external manifestation of what's really going on inside you.

You have decided to take intentional action towards a goal which is done over an extended period of time. A lot of "gears" are turning and you have to be clear that they are in action. It starts with emotional clarity.

When you decide on a goal, this means that you have answered crucial questions. "Is this what I really want? Is this goal worthy of my time and sacrifice? Does this goal line up with my values and my priorities in life?"

Come up with your own list of questions. Regardless, they all have to lead to one place and one place alone: emotional clarity. This is not you daydreaming. Nor is it you being jealous or envious of what your friends desire. This is definitely not the time for you to try to live out your parent's dreams for you. No!

This is you. Your goal must be yours and yours alone. If you're able to answer those questions, then you have reached a point of emotional clarity. And at that point, you have also decided that you will do whatever it takes to achieve that goal.

This means a focus on action. This commitment to action is what separates your goal selection to simple wishing and hoping. All the hoping and wishing in the world is not going to help you get to where you need to go.

You need to take action. This means the goal that you have selected has enough information for you to take action on. In other words, it's self-executing. The moment you decide on it, you would know what to do.

Next, you know your mind and your body are interlocked as far as your goals go when you commit to triggering the set of consequences that will flow from your actions. In other words, you're not just doing stuff to do stuff.

You're focused on getting a certain consequence from your actions because the space between where you are now and your ultimate goal can be a span of several years. Several things have to happen before you reach your goal.

You have to change often times and drastic ways for you to attain your goal. Are you willing to commit to that journey? This requires emotional clarity, a focus on action, and a focus on getting certain consequences of your actions.

Simply filling out a form here, talking about it there, that's not going to work. As you commit each action, it leads to another action with its own consequences. When you're aware of the consequences of your actions, you know how much is expected from you.

You get a clear understanding of what's at stake. This is why it becomes crucial for you to make the right decision at the right time.

DECIDE AND STAND BY IT

Now that you've selected a goal and decided to go for it with everything you've got, you've got to do one more thing. You've got to consciously decide to stand by that decision. This is the ignition point.

What if I told you that rockets going to the moon actually burn up a larger percentage of their fuel as they lift off from the launch pad? How come? This is the point in that long journey where a rocket will face the most opposition.

The earth's gravity is so strong that a rocket has to burn up a large chunk of its fuel just to lift off a few thousand feet in the air. But as it soars higher in the air, it uses less and less fuel.

When you select a goal and decide to go for it with everything that you have and consciously decide to stand by that decision, you burn up a lot of that fuel. This takes willpower because at that point, there's so many things trying to pull you down and hold you back.

In the back of your mind, you will try to sabotage and undermine yourself. Part of you will be doubtful. "Do I really have what it takes? Is this even the right goal? Why should I do that? It seems so hard and takes so much time when I can do something else? Why should I even stay in school when I already have a job offer?"

You will be bombarded with so many choices and a lot of them seem so tempting because you get to enjoy now. As the old saying goes, "Hard work pays off in the future, but laziness pays off instantly."

A lot of that temptation will take the form of a video game console like an Xbox or PlayStation. It can take the form of a boyfriend or a girlfriend. It can take many different forms. But the formula is classic: why go through the pain of a long term commitment when there is a pleasurable shortcut today?

You will need a lot of willpower to get past this liftoff stage because you're going to have to stand by it. I wish I could tell you that this is a one-time big-time kind of thing where you say to yourself "I'm going to stand by my decision."

And when you say that and think it with all its intensity, that's all you need to push you through the next day, the next week, the next month, the next few years.

Unfortunately, it doesn't work that way. You're going to have to stand by that decision. Not even week by week. That would be awesome. No! Not even day by day.

You have to stand by your decision moment by moment. This is the ignition point and this is what builds determination.

Once you start, determination means you keep going

Once you have decided consciously that you will stand by your decision, which is to give your goal everything that you have and sacrifice for it, this means you have to keep going. Again, this is easier said than done.

When you decide on pursuing your goal, what do you think will happen? The internal temptations start to begin. You start doubting. You see what your friends are doing and you wish you could join them.

You go online and before you know it, a minute on Facebook turns into an hour. You try to take a break and you go to Twitter and that 5-minute break turns into 3 hours. There's just so many traps in front of you.

Determination means you keep going forward. This also means overcoming the consequences of your bad planning. Just because you realize that you screwed up on one part of your goal, does this give you an excuse to stop? You know the answer to this.

RELENTLESS DETERMINATION

A lot of people take comfort from the fact that they made bad plans. So they use that as an excuse to stop. Similarly, unforeseen circumstances pop up all the time. Maybe your girlfriend got pregnant. Maybe you got pregnant or your parents got fired or somebody dies.

Whatever the case may be, these unforeseen circumstances can come at you from many different directions and worst of all, there could be black swans. What's a black swan? It is an unforeseen circumstance with exponentially shocking and unpredictable effects.

For instance, you just got admitted to college and you have laid out all the pre-law courses that you're going to be taking. You got straight A's for your first 2 years and things are looking bright because now you're preparing for the law school admission test.

It's a couple of years from now, but you're giving yourself a big lead so you can get a nice head start to get a very high score. Then the financial crash comes. Banks start to fail. Nobody's hiring. Law firms are not hiring. Everybody expects 10 years' experience. And there you are, in your junior year of college, you're not even in law school and you see your future as a partner in a big law firm starting to fade.

You have to keep going. Nobody expected the economy to tank. But you have to keep going. That is determination. What makes this all challenging for a lot of people is one simple fact: great planning can increase the chances of success, but it doesn't guarantee victory.

A lot of dreamers and ambitious people such as yourself think that as long as they cross all their T's and dot all their I's and their plans are all laid out that somehow, someway, this guarantees victory.

Let go of that idea. The best that you can hope for is that when everything is clear, you at least have a fighting chance when it's time to make a detour. When you come in expecting the possibility of the unexpected, at least you are in a better position to be able to handle things when surprises do happen.

At the very least, you're not going to be caught flat-footed or, worse yet, you are not going to lose it. You're not going to panic and think that this is the worst thing ever or it's the end of the world.

Instead, you will be able to make the necessary changes and sacrifices so you can eventually get where you need to go. Yes, it can even take the form of putting your dreams on hold for a few years while you work at a job you don't really like and defer your dream so you can get the resources you need to pursue it later on. Are you willing to do that? Are you willing to suffer? Are you willing to swallow your pride?

Is your goal worthy enough for you to overcome your natural impatience? These are questions only you can answer. Determination keeps you going, oftentimes, in the darkest hour. Imagine for a moment you envisioned you best life, best career, lifestyle and everything that you can imagine, then life hits you in the gut and knocks you to your knees. You can't breathe and you start to see your dreams fading fast. What do you do? What is your course of action?

Are you willing to keep going despite the fact that all these clear lines of your plans became gray overnight? Now, you just feel that there is no certainty up ahead.

You know where you need to go but the money's not there. You have a plan but you got injured or just lost a loved one. My father passed away from cancer in 2014, the next year my grandmother passed; a year later one of my favorite uncles died accidentally. I was devastated from the constant loss of family, yet I had to continue working on Master's degree, carry on a relationship and fulfill work obligations. I knew that my family would want to see me succeed and I could not let them down even though they were no longer here. Can you find the will when you reach deep down inside to keep going at all costs? This is easier said than done.

RELENTLESS DETERMINATION

Determination is the ability to keep pushing ahead regardless of what happens.

Determination means you push forward until you achieve your goal. None of these means you have to do it in a straight line. This doesn't necessarily mean that it's going to happen overnight or even within a reasonable period of time. Determination means you're going to have to be flexible and adaptable.

You have to be flexible in your route, the amount of energy that you need to take, the sacrifices you have to make, and the timeline. Is your dream worth it? Is your dream so worthwhile that you're willing to sacrifice 10 years or more waiting for it?

This means you're able to handle setbacks in such a way that they don't stop you from continuing forward. Determination means you are prepared emotionally for the inevitable detours.

Now, this is easier said than done because being prepared mentally for detours means you don't let your failures and disappointments define you. Maybe, you originally envisioned Harvard Law School or a music career but the way things turned out, you have to wait a longer time, or you have to go to another school.

When I graduated from high school I didn't immediately go college. I wanted to give myself a break and then enter in during the spring semester. As fate would have it, I would have to wait even longer. Shortly after my 18th birthday I was scheduled to start my freshman year at Virginia State University, a historically black college in Petersburg, Virginia. I was so excited and eager to leave home and experience the campus life. I was dating this girl at the time and went to see her the day before I was supposed to leave when my entire life changed forever. There were two guys at her house that I had never seen and apparently one of them was also dating her, which I knew nothing about. We exchanged words, got into a heated argument and a fight broke out while in her kitchen. I ended up getting a second degree burn to my right arm which would leave me scarred for life. My hopes and dreams of college had to be put on hold while I recovered.

The pain that I experienced was excruciating but nothing compared to looking into a mirror and seeing a part of my body physically damaged. Still I summoned the courage and faith to walk onto that campus the very next summer in humid Virginia heat with long sleeves and shorts. The funny thing about it is; all the kids thought I was trying to be preppy and cool, but I was just hiding my scars from the world. I knew I had follow my dreams no matter what, but at 18 years old, I wasn't prepared for the blow that life would give me at that moment. I had to find faith and strength in God to keep moving.

Are you willing to keep going forward? Are you going to let this setback define you or taint your dream? It's so easy to let failure define your life, to give in to excuses. I was once guilty of this too.

You say to yourself, "Well, if I can't marry her, then I'm not going to marry at all," or "I'm not going to fall in love again." You let the disappointment define your project and goal.

Determination also means that you learn to spot other opportunities; you learn to pivot. It turns out that even if you hit a wall, there is a side door that leads to the same place. There might be an alternative route, but this requires time, patience, and mental focus.

Determination also means that you use your time involved waiting for your goal to prepare for your goal instead of just loafing, coasting, or waiting for others to get it together.

What are you preparing for? You are preparing yourself technically. If method A doesn't work now, can it work tomorrow? What about method B? Is there another route? Is there another way?

All of these important skill sets are united by determination because at the end of the day, it is what gives you the power to keep pushing ahead regardless of the setback, the disappointment, the bitterness of failure, the embarrassment, and the act of discouragement of people around you.

People might even think you've lost your mind. Are you willing to keep going forward? That is determination

This book teaches you how to harness the power of determination step-by-step. You will learn the conscientiousness you need to be able to overcome any external circumstance as well as internal doubts and self-sabotage so you can live up to your fullest potential. How do you build determination?

In the following chapters, I'm going to walk you through the following steps:

Step #1. **Delay gratification in everything you do**

Step #2. **Act on the most important things first**

Step #3. **Constantly remind yourself of the purpose you have chosen**

Step #4. **Go for both outcomes and a state of flow**

Step #5. **Change your relationship with your past**

Step #6. **Focus on what you do now**

Step #7. **Be conscious of your sacrifices**

Step #8. **Let your measurement of your success drive your forward**

Step #9. **Call the shots!**

RELENTLESS DETERMINATION

These are the nine steps that you would need to go from fear, indecision, or uncertainty to personal victory. Determination is what pushes you forward. It has to be relentless. It has to be clear-eyed. It has to be focused. The nine steps I'm going to teach you enables you to build up that kind of determination until you become unstoppable.

HOW TO BUILD DETERMINATION

Step #1: Delay gratification in everything you do

Let's get one thing clear. You may be pumped up when you start working towards your goal. It may seem that given the tremendous amount of energy you had when you started, it's only a matter of time until you achieve your goal.

This is what it usually looks like in the beginning. The problem is one day gives way to another day and days started two weeks, weeks turned into months. Before you know it, it seems like your goal is still a long way away.

This is where you'll be tested. This is where you need to develop determination. Most people can get pumped up. They can start with a tremendous amount of energy and almost look like they're pretty much unstoppable. Are these long days when things aren't happening? This will get you to doubt.

Keep in mind that you're not going to doubt your goal. You will still fully believe in them. The problem is, you may doubt that your goal or that the Things you need to do to achieve your ultimate goal are all that important today.

Why? It seems so far off. This is the point in time where you have to be very careful. It's very tempting to just take it easy or coast. You want to put in the least amount of work because it seems that it's going to take a while for your desired result to come.

Why sweat it? Why beat yourself up today? In the back of your mind, you're thinking I'll just put in the bare minimum or I'll just skip work today. Maybe I'll do it tomorrow. I know I can always catch up later on. It's going to be a while.

You may think that you're not doing much of anything or you're not harming yourself or your chances of success when you think this way. You're wrong. Why? You start developing bad habits and those bad habits shape your life.

Determination through delayed gratification is like working out at the gym.

People who have worked out at the gym, lifting weights would know that stressing your muscles are the only way to make them grow. If you haven't worked out before and you hit the weights the first time, you probably would be able to pump some iron.

You might even get a lot of sets out of the way. When the third day comes, your muscles will hurt so bad that it feels like murder. They're aching. If you're not careful, it might seem like you tore a muscle. It doesn't feel good.

At that point, you have two choices. You can take the day off, or the next few days off until the pain goes away. On the other hand, you can go straight back to the gym and apply pressure on those aching muscles, which you think is the right choice. Is that what you think?

When you power through the pain and discomfort, you're training your muscles to withstand a lot more punishment. Almost by a miracle, the pain disappears. You can then continue your workout as long as you have set rest days. Anybody starting out lifting weights at the gym will know this firsthand.

The same applies to delaying gratification. You know, it's going to suck. You know that there are many other things you could do that are more fun and enjoyable, but you have to stick to the job in front of you.

Whether it's hitting the books, going to the gym, doing exercise, listening to your partner's problems, or any other area in your life that requires discipline, you just have to stick to it. Success demands discipline.

If you want your big goals for your relationship, your career, your business, your physical health or weight loss plans to become reality, you're going to have to power through it. It can be painful, annoying, challenging, but you have to do it.

What's the worst thing that you can do? Procrastinate or coast. You've decided to do the least amount of work possible and maybe reduce even that to a lower level tomorrow and then the day after that.

Maybe you're even thinking of just putting it off indefinitely. All of these lead to dead ends. Your resolve becomes weaker and weaker. You're destroying your determination when you do this. Thankfully there is a solution.

Solution

If you're having a tough time doing what you need to do in front of you and the temptation to procrastinate seems all but irresistible, do this little trick. Penalize yourself with push-ups.

This would wake you up physically. If you still want to slack or you're still taking your time, do push-ups again.

You end up physically reminding yourself of the test that you need to do right here right now. Throw yourself into that test. Knock it out of the park.

Give it everything you've got. Once you're able to do that, reward yourself with the treat if you wipe out your complete to-do list.

What to do if you take a shortcut?

Let me tell you. When you take a shortcut, you develop a bad habit. Sure, it gets the job done but barely. Whatever success you accomplish, taking the shortcut is shallow. Why? Shortcuts don't allow you to learn what you need to learn.

You have to understand that you're not just learning a task here. You're not just trying to produce an outcome at a certain point in time. You're working on something more important.

You're developing your character.

By doing things the way they should be done according to the highest standards and putting in real work, you develop your character. A good character is a person who lives up to the highest standards and doesn't take shortcuts. You don't compromise.

When you take a shortcut today, this can easily turn into a habit. At the back of your mind you're thinking, well, there's always a shortcut so I may do that. Maybe you might even get the idea that you're being clever.

What you're doing is you're cheating yourself out of the rock-hard character you need to develop. This is the character of a person who will do whatever is necessary to get the job done right the first time around.

Solution

If you find yourself thinking of taking a shortcut, push yourself to do things the hard way, but motivate yourself as you go through the process. How?

Constantly think of how you can streamline the things that you're doing. You know you're doing things the hard way and to the highest standards. Congratulations!

As you do that, see if you can streamline what you're doing to get the same results and produce the same quality, but with less work. Eventually, you will be able to connect the dots.

You will be able to come up with a high-efficiency solution that doesn't compromise the quality of your output, while at the same time reducing the amount of time, labor, and focus you invest. You end up enhancing your productivity and your skills.

What if you stop?

As I mentioned earlier, hard work pays dividends, but laziness robs you now. What do you do when you take a break and you are about to stop the task that you're doing? Maybe you're about to slack off for the rest of the day.

The solution? Focus on what you are going to be losing. You're not motivated by the things you stand to gain. You're not excited about achieving your ultimate goal.

In the back of your mind, it's so distant that the instant payoff of slacking off today completely outweighs whatever rewards your goal has to offer. You just want to stop.

Focus on what you will lose if you do that. Focus on lost time, the lost discipline, and the lost momentum. Concentrate on the fact that you're going to have to relearn a lot of things because you've decided to stop.

Sure, you get to slack off, but you're going to have to start from square one. You don't resume where you left off. Let that sink in. Just think about how hard it is to get back in the gym once you slack off. Allow yourself to be afraid. Allow yourself to be frustrated about having to redo things.

As much as it is a hassle to do what you need to do now, it's much better than slacking off and having to start from square one later on.

Realize that whatever your short term "fixes" will get worse over time.

Whether you decide to stop, stop and slack off or take a shortcut or coast, understand that these temporary "fixes" will scale up over time. Mark my words. They will come back to bite you in the ass eventually.

What happens when you automatically take those actions when confronted with any kind of resistance, challenge, objections, or discouragement as you work towards your goal?

The answer should be obvious. You get weaker and weaker. Your willpower dissipates over time.

As a result, you don't train your mind to respond effectively and in your ignorance real solutions will start to bite you.

You'll become mentally weaker and more impatient. Before you know it, you feel entitled to things to be easy and manageable. You can only handle so much responsibility, so much pressure, and so much risk.

What do you think this all translates to? Again, this is obvious. You get less reward because too many other people are doing the same thing.

Very few are doing the hard work and investing the right amount of time, focus, and sacrifice to meet their goals. They are the ones who end up with the big payday. Everybody else is left with the crumbs.

Focus on what you will gain.

If you're able to apply the solutions discussed above, you need to focus on what you gained. It's not just a question of allowing your fears to help you stay determined, instead of slacking off.

Unless you consciously focus on what you're gaining, you're going to lose the lesson.

Before you know it, it becomes more and more tempting to just slack off. You will start bargaining with yourself and come up with all sorts of excuses why it's not a big deal if you stop (initially temporarily) on your way to your big goals.

You have to be conscious of what you're gaining when you override the natural tendency to slack off, take a shortcut or coast. What are you getting? First of all, you're able to withstand temptation. Congratulate yourself. This is a big victory.

Every single time you withstand temptation, your willpower gets stronger and stronger. You're investing in your resistance to temptation. This means you're able to delay gratification today for quick and easy payoffs in exchange for greater victories down the road.

You also learn to build, work, and act based on your highest values and standards. Never underestimate this. Why? If you're ever in any study group or work group, you will see a pattern.

Excellent students and employees operate with the highest standards. They hold themselves up to metrics of excellence, other people wish they had. You're able to do this because you refuse to slack off, coast, take it easy, or use a shortcut.

In the back of your mind, you're thinking, I know I am capable of better. I know that deep down inside I'm capable of so much more. Why should I allow myself to settle for "good enough"? I am excellent. I am the best. I have what it takes.

This is a very important reward to work for. Next, you should focus on the fact that you gained patience and resilience. It takes inner strength to overcome the temptation of just slacking off or doing something pleasurable. Work is a hassle.

To many people, it might even seem like a daily humiliation, but you power it through anyways. You work deeply in the moment. You allow yourself to enjoy yourself as you solve puzzle after puzzle which triggers the next thing that you gain.

You're able to build creativity. The problem with people who are always looking for a shortcut or an easy way out is they cheat themselves of their natural ability to find resourceful solutions you know that you're going to have to work hard.

It doesn't necessarily mean that you have to do the task in the most backbreaking or mind-bending way. Maybe there are patterns there.

Attacking this problem set long enough and you might be able to come up with better results, greater productivity without breaking a sweat. How come? You tapped into your imagination and creativity.

Whether you look at delaying gratification from the perspective of rewards or punishments, the conclusion is obvious. You need to develop this trait if you want to achieve the big goals you have set for yourself in your life. There are no shortcuts.

Step #2: Act on the most important things first

On a given day, if you were to ask the typical American employee to detail everything they did, you'd be shocked. On paper, it seems that they're very busy. They're calling this person. They're going to this meeting. They're checking out this important email, so on and so forth.

If you were to boil it all down into activities that produced a profit for the company, you'd be lucky if eight hours yield one hour of productive work. It is surprising, right? Don't be. The reason why you should not be all that amazed is that this is how the human mind works.

We tend to fill our days with fluff. We'd rather look busy or feel that we're busy than work on the stuff that matters.

It's no surprise then that the American workplace is getting more and more stressful year after year. When people focus on doing busy work or doing things just for the sake of doing things and they're just deploying their bodies.

These are not just a physical set of actions. They're also stressed out. In many cases, they're emotionally tapped out. In the back of their minds, they're thinking, well if this is so emotionally draining and stressful, then this means that I am getting stuff done. Wrong.

It's easy to get lost in the weeds. The Pareto Principle, also known as the 80/20 rule states, that 20% of the things you do account for 80% of your results. To make progress you must understand the Pareto Principle applies to your work just like most other human activities.

Knowing this, it's no shock that most employees only managed to turn in one hour of real productive work for every eight hours of their presence at the office. How do you fix this?

So how do you fix this problem?

You just have to be more mindful of the things that you are doing. Each action that you take must be directly linked to your biggest goals.

If your goals can be broken down into sub-goals and those sub-goals can be broken down into smaller goals, which in turn can yield daily tasks, there has to be a straight line from those daily tasks to your biggest goals.

If you don't see the connection, then that daily task in front of you is not worth prioritizing. Pick an action item that is a more direct "investment" in the realization of your biggest goals and aspirations.

This should be your North Star. You should ask yourself when you are doing a task; is what I'm prioritizing going to directly lead me to my biggest life goals? It's that simple.

If the answer is no, then set that aside and look for the task that is directly connected to your life goal. Once those are over and done with, you can then take the other stuff.

Be aware of the impact of your action. When you make it a point to first focus on doing tasks that are directly related to your big goals, you are allowing yourself to be clear on the consequences of your actions. Using this philosophy, everything you do has a point.

You're not wasting the precious hours of your life engaged in meaningless nonsense. Look around you. The vast majority of people are engaged in meaningless nonsense. They take care of that stuff today. Guess what?

There's more of that tomorrow, the day after, the week after, the month after, and the year after. It can go on and on. Is that what you want your life's work to be?

If you're able to wrap your head around this and you're able to prioritize meaningful tasks, allow yourself to get emotionally engaged. Allow yourself to think I am doing something important. I am doing something purposeful.

The more conscious you are of the connection of what you're doing now to the big goals that you would like to realize in the future, the more empowered you become. Your determination becomes stronger.

It turns out that you're not just spinning your wheels. This all has a point. If you keep this up, this culminates into a sense that you are in control.

Unlike most people, you're not chasing your tail nor are you allowing yourself to be driven by external circumstances beyond your control. No, none of that is happening. Instead, every single decision you make and purposeful action you take leads to a big payoff.

A payoff that you chose. Isn't that enough to pump you up? Isn't that an emotional realization that this is going on enough to steal your resolve to make it day after day?

Redraw the connection between your decisions and your desires. Every single day, you should write down what your big desire in life is. Remind yourself of your big goals and objectives every single day. Focus on those goals you've written down.

Draw in your mind a clear straight line between the things that you're going to be doing today, and that crowning achievement of personal victory in the future. Do you see the connection?

RELENTLESS DETERMINATION

Do you see the little things you're doing now starting a chain reaction that ultimately leads to where you want to go? If the answer is no, then look at your other tasks until you see the connection.

When you can connect what you choose to do in the here and now to what you want to see happen in the future, you get a sense of certainty.

It all sinks in and becomes clear. I have power over my life. I can select my future by taking this road and not that road or avoiding what I do normally and instead of doing this. I will be able to turn that idea that I've always had into a reality that I can see touch and experience.

If this doesn't work for you, and you're not pumped up, flip the script. Think about what would happen if you chose to do what seems like everybody else does. They put their futures in the hands of other people. They pursue goals that other people have set for them.

They find themselves chasing after objectives put in place by people they can't control. They sense the powerlessness, lack of direction, and frustration. Allow this to sink in. I want you to get triggered.

I want you to stoke the fires of your determination for a moment by realizing: I don't want to live that kind of life. That's how I used to live in the past. I want power over my life. I want to call the shots. I want to live in a world I made. I am the author of my destiny.

Be clear about the relationship between the small stuff and the big stuff. As I've mentioned earlier, 20% of the things you do produce 80% of your results. Focus on that 20%, the rest is fluff. This doesn't mean that you can conveniently neglect the 80% or forget about them.

No. Knock out the 20% first and once you have taken care of that, focus on the small stuff. If you follow this sequence, you will be able to master the big stuff. Why? That requires your willpower.

That's the hard stuff that you've been trying to avoid. You want to coast. You want to find a shortcut. You want to slack, or you just want to quit. That's why the big stuff is hard.

It takes it out of you. The good news is, every single day that you do the big stuff first and knock it out for that day, your resolve gets stronger and stronger. Before you know it, you don't even hesitate. It is no longer a hassle.

Here's the secret, once you have reached that level of inner strength and determination, the small stuff becomes ridiculously easy. Think about it. You tackle the giant that you've been trying to avoid all this time.

Better yet you made it a habit to knock out the giant first thing in the morning. Everything else is child's play. Seriously. Focus on the big stuff first, because you're building many different skill sets while you're doing that.

Everything else pretty much takes care of itself. If you're able to knock out the stuff that you'd rather dance around, avoid, evade, or kick down the road, you will demolish the small stuff with no problem.

REMEMBER YOUR WHY

As you make your way to your ultimate goal, it can become a very lonely trip. In fact, at many points in your journey, don't be surprised if you ask yourself, "Why am I even doing this? Why is it that everybody has it easier than me? Am I just making things harder on myself by holding myself to a higher standard or going this specific path? It seems that everybody around is happier because they've taken a shortcut."

These questions are very easy to blow off in the beginning. Earlier, were very idealistic, and you could see the bright contours of your dream. In fact, you're hungry and highly motivated. But as one day gives way to another day, and one week gives way to another week, it starts feeling like it's a grind. It seems that no matter how hard you try and how many problems you overcome, very little seems to change.

When you climb the corporate ladder, it seems that no matter how well you do your job, you don't really get the appreciation that you deserve. It seems that for all your hard work, attention to detail and dedication, it all falls between the cracks because you work at this massive, faceless, anonymous corporation.

In fact, it even seems like it's all stacked against you because the ones who get promoted tend to know people who were promoted before them. It's as if everybody is moving up as part of this little club, and guess what? You're not a member of that club. What are you going to do? What are you going to think?

It is precisely in these moments, which often stretch for long periods of time that you have to stay laser-focused on your purpose. Please understand that this purpose is not entrusted to you by somebody else. It didn't drop in your lap nor did you stumble upon it. No. This purpose is something that you have actually chosen. It is a reminder of the fact that you own your life and that you are in control of it.

Ask yourself, "Why am I doing this?" Remind yourself of why you started this journey. You have to be clear about the reasons. You have to walk through the different levels of reasons you have, and understand that it must lead to the same place. It's okay to be confused at first but, ultimately, the purpose you have chosen for yourself must line up with the ultimate need most human beings have.

Abraham Maslow's Hierarchy of Needs describes a multilevel series of needs that motivate people. At the most basic, we need to eat, drink, and have some sort of shelter. We also need security so nobody harms us. However, once we meet these needs, we're still needy. There's something missing. At this point, you're looking for a way to assert yourself, to expand who you are and achieve status.

This doesn't necessarily have to be a bad thing. All this means is that you have some sort of rank in society. Once these are met, then these are replaced by higher needs like the love for family, a sense of service to something bigger than you. This also includes a sense of honor that arises from your membership in a group. This sense of duty can involve sacrifice.

In other words, you define yourself not so much by your selfish needs or your family members, but you start thinking of yourself as part of something bigger like a greater community or a nation, and this level of commitment can take the form of sacrificing your life for something higher like the nation. In all of these, there's a strong emotional bond. You might even define your personal pride as the ability to sacrifice for the greater good.

Once this is established, the highest level of needs that people have, according to Maslow, is a sense of transcendence. In other words, you have a sense of personal destiny, that you're not just an accident, and that your life is not just this fluke that flashed into existence. Your life goals actually have an impact when it comes to history.

You need to go through these different levels when answering the one question that will crop up again and again as you make your way through your journey. "Why am I doing this?" Alternatively, you might ask, "What is the point to all of this?"

However, if you go through those different levels, you would see that you're doing this because of your destiny. There is something to you that's special. You are here for a very important reason. So, focus on your purpose and go through these levels, and you will end up with a strong emotional and intellectual boost

If anything, you will see that you're not the typical person who's just doing things for the sake of doing things. You'd be surprised as to how many people go on certain career paths because they think that's what is expected of them. They didn't choose that path. It's as if they're living their lives on auto-pilot. The same applies to relationships, social circles, even hobbies. Many people do get good at these areas. You can tell by their eyes that there's something missing.

You're not one of those people. You've chosen your purpose, so you need to remember it in the proper context. It's not enough that it makes you feel good. Instead, remember it and frame it within the context of personal destiny.

Don't Stick with Affirmations of Purpose

It's very tempting to come up with some sort of shortcut for your personal purpose and say, "Well, I was born to do this" or "This is who I am." That's great. There's something missing. These affirmations of purpose are shallow, and when you're faced with a lot of resistance, boredom, confusion or flat-out discouragement, these affirmations are not enough, sad to say. You're not going to be up to the job. You're going to fall flat.

In fact, don't be surprised if you say an affirmation of purpose and you quickly forget it because of the heat of the moment. You're frustrated, disappointed. You might even be upset with yourself as to why you made certain decisions. Affirmations in that context don't really do much good.

This is why you need to visualize your purpose. Put simply, don't just give it lip service. Don't be content with just reducing it into mere words. You have to take the next step.

Visualize Your Purpose

Since you've done the intellectual and emotional heavy lifting, of going through Maslow's several levels of human needs as described above, the next step is to go beyond mere words. You have to see these words.

Imagine yourself living out your destiny. What would it look like? What will you be surrounded by when you have arrived at your life's purpose? Who will you surrounded by when you live your dream?

Usually, at this point, you will feel a rush of emotions. You can't help but be determined because you're truly pumped up. Oftentimes, when people do this in the midst of all the discouragement, pain, depression and sense of loss or confusion, they can't help but feel a massive surge of energy. Imagine yourself in that moment and internalize.

Allow yourself to feel that. Focus on the details. Allow yourself to get emotionally transported. Make every single time you do this as intense as the first time.

To make things "stick" emotionally, experience that scene in three dimensions. What I mean by that is don't just focus on what you can see. Imagine what it would sound like. Think about what you can touch and how it would feel. Try to wrap your head around the possible tastes and scents involved. When you experience something in 3D, which engages all five of your senses, it's as if you're living that moment. This is crucial to fully emotionally accepting and then becoming that which you focus on.

What should you expect? The shallowest is that it feels good, but let me tell you, feeling good is not going to get you from point A to point B. instead, you should focus on the sense of urgency. If you're able to experience this in 3D with all your senses, then you know it's real. You're not just wasting your time, and you're definitely not just going through the motions.

Allow yourself to be pushed by that sense of urgency so you can remain determined. If your determination is flagging, or if it seems like you have hit one wall after another, this sense of urgency will make you punch through.

Go Beyond Emotionally Connecting with Your Purpose

The next stage, once you've bathed in that sense of urgency, is to transcend. In other words, focus on the fact that your purpose is your destiny. This is what you were made for. This is what you're about. Wrap your mind and your heart around the idea that this is your personal need. This is the reason why you're alive.

You may be thinking to yourself, "Wow, that's a bit shallow because my main purpose in life is to become a very wealthy person." If this is in fact your main goal, then you will have to put in the work.

To amass wealth generally means earning it, and how do you earn money? You provide value to people whether in the form of haircuts or other services or goods like merchandise? You have something that they need so they give you something of value for what they need. Value for value.

This requires becoming a different person because all of us are trained to take, take, and take. For you to earn money, you have to learn how to give what the market wants. This is not easy because there are many competitors so you would have to learn what the market needs. It takes a while. There's a lot of risk.

You have to be brave. You have to be courageous. Oftentimes, your capital starts to dwindle. In fact, in many cases, you go into debt. However, you solve problems on a day-to-day basis and, before you know it, it starts to scale and your business expands.

Businesses are personal challenges. They force people to become problem solvers and the business journey also forces people to overcome their natural tendencies towards greed, taking shortcuts, or coasting.

This is why relatively few businesses become very big successes because most people aren't willing to put in the kind of sacrifice and focus needed for great success. If business success is your ultimate purpose, then understand that this is not just about making money. Far from it.

It's about becoming a different person and overcoming your fears. Make that your personal mantra. In that context, your personal vision is "I am an overcomer and problem solver. I create new worlds based on other people's problems. Other people have needs and gaps and holes in their lives. My purpose is to solve those problems."

Don't focus on the fact that when everything is said and done, you become a very wealthy person. That's gravy. The real reward is the fact that you are able to help and create things that weren't there before.

Make that your personal mantra. This goes beyond emotionally connecting with your purpose. This reaches deeper because this is ultimately who you are.

How Do You Know You're Succeeding?

If you go through all the process of reminding yourself of the purpose you have chosen and connecting yourself with that purpose and ultimately defining your meaning around that, how do you know you're on the right track? Very simple: there will be results.

For everything else, I hate to say it, but you were just spinning your wheels. Why? You didn't live out this connection between emotion, purpose, and action. It all boils down to emotion plus action.

If you really define yourself as an overcomer or a person who brings out excellence or pursues excellence and that's how you define your personal meaning, you're not just going to go to the gym and go through the motions.

What would you expect to gain with that attitude? When you train, you lose your breath. You go all in. You find every last ounce of energy as you push that heavy weight off your chest. That's the intensity at which you train not only in the gym but also in life.

Alternatively, if we're using a business example, you're not going to sleep if you know that your business is struggling and not making as much money as it could be. You focus on a specific problem that is causing the lackluster or mediocre revenues, and you keep hammering at it until you come up with a solution. You then try one solution after another until you find the one that works the best and guess what? Once you see that it's working, you pour even more of your profits into it to scale it up to take it to its furthest logical extreme. You explore newer territory. You look for new opportunities.

This is the difference between purpose-driven action and people who are just using purpose statements to make the sense of uncertainty and security and fear go away. I hope you can see the difference.

What is the bottom line? Your purpose changes your actions. You're not going to settle for doing what you used to do before.

Similarly, purpose changes how you look at time. It is very tempting to look at time as inexhaustible. After all, you made it this far. There's a lot of time left on the clock.

You may not have much money. You may not have much physical energy. However, in your mind, you're thinking, "Well, at least I have a lot of time." Wrong!

If you are working with a deep sense of purpose and destiny, every second counts. In fact, every single moment is precious because it's that moment that could lead to a breakthrough. Why are you not taking full advantage of that time? Why are you not rolling up your sleeves and getting down to business - whether it's working out at the gym, working on your relationships, studying in school, getting your business going, or taking your career to the next level. Real purpose-driven living delivers results.

Step #4: Go for both outcomes and a state of flow.

Has this ever happened to you: you're working on something that you normally find difficult, for whatever reason, this time around, it seems like everything just falls into place?

As you go through your work, everything seems clear. It doesn't matter how hard this project seemed to you before. Everything you try and all the directions you go lead to a big payoff.

A lot of people think that when this happens to them, they're just lucky. They would describe work as consisting of good days and bad days. This is one of the good days.

The truth is, when things become seem easy to you, it's because you have reached a state of flow. This is when you are challenged but at the same time, your resourcefulness, creativity, cleverness, and imagination are all engaged.

You're able to knock out the problem in a sustained way. The challenge doesn't disappear, but you are up to the job. This whole process engages you at all levels. We're talking intellectual, emotional, and psychological.

Your engine is now firing on all cylinders and things are moving. When you look back, you would notice that what you're doing is far from easy.

Normally you would have a tough time with that task but at certain times, things just come to you. Unfortunately, a lot of people are under the impression that this just happens by luck.

They happen to be in the right frame of mind at a certain point in time, and things just happened. They have a fairly passive view of this mental, intellectual and emotional state.

You can control your state of flow

What if I told you that you can trigger the state of flow on command? It isn't easy but if you tackle your day to day tasks with the right frame of mind, it's more likely that you would achieve a state of flow than otherwise.

Too many people think that achieving a state of flow isn't necessary. After all, they're working a job. Who's going to benefit? It's not them. It's their boss. Who wants to do that?

As I've repeatedly said in this book, a lot of people just want to do the bare minimum, while trying to maximize the rewards that they get. Intentionally achieving a state of flow for the benefit of your employer runs counter to this very common idea.

In other words, you just want to put in a minimal amount of work, just so you can get the reward that you're used to. Why? It's to intentionally trigger your state of flow.

Let states of flow become part of your desired outcomes

Generally speaking, when people set up goals, they look at rewards. They see themselves in a big house, going on frequent vacations all over the world, and just enjoying the very best that life has to offer.

This is a reward mindset. The idea is you work hard, you sacrificed enough and there you are, you have arrived. You deserve everything you have coming to you.

RELENTLESS DETERMINATION

While this is important as a source of motivation, please understand that for you to achieve these things, you have to become a different person. Your journey has to change you.

It is really important to understand that when you define your life rewards in terms of money, awards, acclaim, fame, and other common measurements, it's simply not enough.

Keep this in mind when you go for certain outcomes. You'd be surprised as to how much of a letdown they would be on many levels. You're emotionally let down. It doesn't feel as intense as you thought.

Ultimately you don't feel all rewarded. If you're not careful, don't be surprised if you come away thinking, okay, is that all there is to it. Now, what?

Given the tremendous amount of sacrifice that you need to make to reach certain goals, it's very easy to just say, so what? It's kind of like that phrase in the famous Linkin Park song, "In the end, it didn't matter."

You don't want to find yourself in that position. To increase your level of determination, reframe your outcomes in terms of the state of flow.

Let your measurement of success be the process

Instead of thinking about the kind of goodies that you would end up with and how much money you would have or what kind of title you will attain, think of the process.

Define your outcomes in terms of how often you will achieve a state of flow. If you're able to do this, you become super-competent in a relatively short period. Why?

You achieve a state of flow because you tackle high level and often difficult tasks. You increase your discipline. You focus on the most challenging tasks first.

RELENTLESS DETERMINATION

Instead of running away from it because you're scared or you're afraid of failure, you run towards it. You can't help but get excited about the new puzzle that you would solve today.

If you're able to keep this up over an extended period, you will scale up your effectiveness. You enhance your ability to solve problems by tapping into your unlimited amount of imagination, creativity, and resourcefulness.

This is how you position yourself to go from victory to victory. This must be part of how you define success. At the end of the day, it's the experiences that people appreciate the most.

If you don't believe me when was the last time you bought something really nice for yourself? Maybe it's a nice car or it's a nice bag that has the label Prada or Louie Vuitton on it.

Chances are when you first bought that item, you were excited. You couldn't wait to show it to your friends or to be seen with that item. Whether it's a car or a piece of a luxury item, like a bag or clothing, it's all the same.

You want to be seen with it. It's a big part of who you are. It makes you feel complete. It even makes you feel like you're somebody.

After a while, once you'd noticed that other people have that same item, it's hold-on-you starts to weaken. Before you know it, you're back to square one. While it's true, that buying stuff can deliver a certain measure of happiness, it doesn't last long.

It's like an emotional or psychological sugar high. It's real. It can be intense, but it has a very short shelf life. It dissipates fairly quickly. If you're not careful, your credit card bills remain. It's much better to focus on experiences.

Experiences become part of you. When you catch up with friends of yours from 10 years ago, you probably would talk about stuff that you did together. Guess what?

When you add up the dollars and cents of that particular activity or memory, it doesn't cost much money. Since you hang on to that memory, it means so much to you.

It might define part of who you are. It has enriched you. This is the power of memory and this is how precious memory is. I want you to apply that to your journey.

As you go through the process of triggering a state of flow, define your journey based on your ability to trigger that state of flow and the amazing problem-solving experiences that you enjoy while you go through it.

Eventually, if you keep this up and you look forward to achieving that state, you end up crushing your challenges. They may first start as scary and intimidating, but eventually, you start looking forward to them.

You start seeing them as puzzles. They're no longer soul-draining, headache-inducing problems. Instead, they're fun challenges.

When you go through one state of flow after another, your competence ratchets up along with your emotional familiarity with problem-solving.

The reason why a lot of people struggle with their jobs is that they've already mastered the work. It's like the back of their hand. They know it backward and forwards. They're not challenged so it has low engagement.

While they can do it with blindfolds on, they remain stuck. Why? They don't want to try something harder. What for? I don't want to just make my boss richer when he already is.

They remain stuck. They get bored. Do you think that they're growing when they find themselves in that competence holding pattern? Of course not.

Just like with your muscles, if you don't constantly challenge them or put pressure on them, they start to get weak. If you decide to take a break, where one cheat day becomes a cheat week, and a cheat week becomes a cheat month, your muscles get softer and softer.

Before you know it, you're back to square one. Your body looks exactly like the way it did before you started working out.

Focus on achieving states of flow

When you make it your daily goal to achieve a state of flow, you deepen your level of intellectual and emotional engagement and you increase the quality of your work.

Ultimately, states of flow lead to deep work. This is work that isn't ministerial. This is the stuff that you know already. This doesn't involve "busy work".

Instead, deep work enables you to look at what you're doing on a day to day basis and come up with alternatives that would take your results to a whole other level. This is where disruptive innovations often take place.

As I mentioned earlier, 80% of the things you do only accounted for 20% of your results. When you're doing deep work, you focus on the 20% and grow it. By just doubling that 20% to 40% on a day to day basis, you add 60% to your total production.

In other words, you go from 100% to 160%. This is how you develop continuous improvement. Deep work looks at the foundation of what you're doing. You're not just looking at how to connect the dots or surface technicalities.

Instead, you think deeply about the tasks that you do on a day to day basis. Knowing this principle, you then ask, why does this work the way it does? Are there other alternatives? Can this principle be applied in different contexts?

That's how your mind would think. This opens up a wide vista of alternatives and opportunities. Throughout it all, there's this fun sense of constant experimentation.

Your job never gets old, because it's filled with explorations and in a sense of possibility and adventure. When you transform your attitude towards work along these lines, your determination deepens.

It is now built on a solid bedrock of competence. Once you develop competence, you would also develop self-confidence. This is the kind of self-confidence nobody can take away from you because you earned it. You built it yourself.

Unfortunately, a lot of kids nowadays are given a trophy just for showing up. Life doesn't work that way. There are no participation trophies in life. You have to earn your way forward.

When you focus on achieving states of flow as part of the outcomes you desire on a day to day basis, this experience will transform you. Not only you become a more competent person, but you would have real self-confidence.

You're not faking it until you make it. It's built on the solid bedrock of your real ability to figure things out and get things done.

NEVER LOOK BACK

Let me ask you if you're running a race and you have a massive rubber band around your waist pulling you back, are you going to get to your goal on time? Are you going to reach your goal at all?

Believe it or not a lot of people who have tried to work towards a grand objective or some sort of big goal for their life allowed their past to drag them back and hold them down. Even if they were able to develop an almost superhuman level of determination, they're just making things harder on themselves.

You don't need to do that because determination involves driving forward. It means fueling your efforts at overcoming what you need to overcome to get to your goal. However, when you have this force dragging you back and holding you, you spend all this time and energy only to settle for a few steps forward. Granted you're still making forward progress, but can you imagine how much further you could have gone if you didn't have this thing holding you back?

You need to pay attention to your past. More specifically, you need to develop the right mindset with your past because if you don't, you're just making things harder on yourself. Am I saying that success would be nearly impossible? Of course not. It's just going to be more difficult. You're going to be spending energy that you didn't have to.

This could have been the kind of willpower and focus that you could have invested in other things. If anything, without the baggage of the past holding you back, you might have achieved your goals sooner rather than later.

So, how do you deal with this? How do you neutralize the effect of the past on your present action? Please pay attention to the following.

Embrace All of You

It's very easy to embrace and celebrate our successes and victories. In fact, we already do this. We think back to the awards we've won or the major accomplishments that we have achieved. It's easy to focus on the good stuff.

The problem is there is more to us than the things that we care to celebrate. We all make mistakes, and those bad choices often have consequences. It is no surprise that a lot of us are embarrassed and often feel humiliated about these past bad calls. Welcome to the club. Nobody's perfect. At some point in the past, you probably have made a bad decision, and it has probably turned at least a few aspects of your life into problematic areas to say the least.

It's very easy to see people's lives consisting of a lot of bright corners, but behind these bright corners are dark alleys filled with shadows. They'd rather not talk about them because they're so embarrassed or it brings so much pain, humiliation, and fear. I grew up in a family full of alcoholics on both sides. Most of the men in my family never accomplished much nor had anything to be proud of and goals were something that didn't exist. They were simply trying to survive the best they knew how and never looked outside of their environment as far as I knew. This is a fact that I don't share with a lot of people due to the negative and painful memories. I had to come to grips with this so I could embrace who I am and so do you.

Make no mistake those things are still part of you and one of the best ways to overcome the negative hold the past has on your life today is to embrace all of you. This means accepting both your successes and also your more 'difficult' memories. At the very least this means reinterpreting your relationship with the past.

Learn to Let Go

When you reinterpret the relationship you have with the past, this doesn't mean you pretend that certain facts never existed. They are facts. They happen.

What's important is that you acknowledge that these happened and that you refuse to deny them. Equally important is that you understand that you have a relationship with your past. It doesn't matter whether you like it or not. It just is.

The good news is it doesn't have to be a negative relationship. By learning to embrace all of yourself, you learn how to let go of the past pain, disappointment, and sub-optimal ways of coping you have developed over the years.

In other words, you acknowledge that these things happened, but you're going to let go of how you've dealt with them. These are two totally different things. You're not letting go of the facts. You're not engaged in some sort of selective and intentional amnesia. You're not doing any of that. Instead, you're focusing on how you responded to those facts.

As you probably already know, constantly getting triggered and feeling disappointed, depressed, discouraged, anxious, and angry every time you think about a past memory or if you encounter something that triggers that memory is not productive. In fact, it weighs you down. It is one of the heavy burdens that you're carrying as you push towards your life's goal. You undermine your overall determination when you hang on to these coping mechanisms. These are not optimal.

You must have a point of clarity where you explicitly say to yourself, 'I chose to react this way in the past, but I also see that they are dead ends. They don't do any good. Sure, there is some sort of emotional payoff but I pay a very high price for that payoff. I can murder the people who have hurt me in my mind all I want, but that emotional satisfaction is psychological cancer. I may have the moral high ground when I paint myself as some sort of victim in my mind but, at the end of the day, all I have in my hands are the ruins of what I could have been.'

I need you to think along these lines and understand what is at stake. Obviously, people don't engage in any kind of activity unless there's something in it for them. There is, believe it or not, something in it for you when you drag back all those negative memories and you choose to cope with them in a certain way. You know it's negative. You know you're not really moving forward emotionally. You know you're not engaged in any kind of self-therapy. However, it is cathartic to a certain extent. It feels good to be a victim.

You have to draw a line somewhere and make peace with all of that and let go. Then and only then will you be able to refuse your past to define you. Get rid of its hold. Get rid of the warped coping mechanisms that you've developed all these years. Maybe they have served some purpose in the past but not now. You have bigger fish to fry. Keep your eyes on the ultimate prize. Believe it or not you are more than your pain, loss, embarrassment, humiliation, emotional abuse, sexual abuse, physical abuse, all that. You are more than that.

It doesn't matter how many people you point your finger to. Ultimately, you're going to have to decide today. Enough! I own all of myself, and I embrace all of myself and, yes, there are facts from my past that I'm not all that proud of. They used to bring me a lot of pain, but they are part of me and I embrace all of me, and I'm going to move forward. Is this going to be easy? Of course not! Is this going to happen overnight? Are you kidding? But it is absolutely necessary. You need to cross that river.

Stop the Blame Game and Take Responsibility

This is where a lot of people get touchy. Can you imagine going through all this abuse, loss, and pain and being told, 'Okay, that happened. I'm sorry that happened,' but you're going to have to stop blaming others and take responsibility for your situation. The all-too-human response is, 'haven't I suffered enough? I'm the one who was the victim here. I'm the one who got beat up on. I'm the one who lost out, who suffered. Who are you to tell me I have to move on?'

However, you have to say it to yourself. Even if we agree that nobody else has the right to tell you to do that, you're going to have to step up and do it because you have to understand that the more you blame others for your past, the more powerless you become. Let that sink in.

If you look at the logic of blaming other people, then it necessarily follows that since they caused the pain, they need to fix it. See how impossible this is? You can't control them. It's hard enough trying to change yourself. Can you imagine trying to change other people that you cannot control?

In fact, if you were to confront them, a lot of them have moved on. Indeed, many of them may have even completely forgotten about that painful thing they did to you. What then?

Stop waiting on other people to get their act together. Stop waiting on other people to 'save' you. That's not going to happen. If they harmed you, chances are they probably harmed other people. You will only find yourself in this ridiculous situation of trying to get some sort of emotional and moral redress from these people, but you have to wait in line. In fact, you probably would need to take a number because they harmed other people in the past.

You have to take care of yourself now and stop blaming them. Instead, take responsibility. Sure, they caused the harm. Nobody's disputing that. Your father abandoned you. Your mother emotionally abused you by calling you ugly. Your boss humiliated you. I can go on and on about whatever your specific past issues may be.

However, at some point, you're going to have to say, 'Enough! I'm going to stop responding like a victim. While I may not have caused this problem, I have power over how I respond, and I'm going to respond in such a way that this doesn't drag me back and hold me down as I move towards my goal.' Focus on what you can do now, and this is the most empowering part. This is the best news. You always have a choice on how to respond.

If you notice that your past coping mechanism only ends up with you feeling small, powerless, marginalized, or even impotent, maybe it's high time that you try responding in a different way. Respond in a way that builds your determination. Respond in a way that highlights your sense of self-ownership. Nobody can take that away from you.

In fact, when you choose to respond this way, you build up your character. You become rare. Why? I hate to say it, but too many people would like to play the victim. They'd like to say to themselves, 'Why do I need to change when I'm the one who suffered? I'm the one who lost out. I'm the one who was left behind. So, people owe it to me. The worlds owes me.' They can then turn around and say, 'Well, the world is unfair.'

Believe me claiming that moral high ground can be very addictive, but you also rob yourself of the power to shape your life right here right now. You can't expect the world to change on your behalf. It turns on its own axis. It's got more than enough of its own problems. It's definitely not going to stop to solve yours. You have to take care of yourself. You have to step up.

That's why so many people allow their pasts to defeat them. In fact, those demons from the past consistently come up and rob them of their victories. Talk about snatching defeat from the jaws of victory. People do this all the time. It's called 'self-sabotage'.

Enough! I want you to say, 'Enough!' because you have better things going for you. You have bigger rewards. Don't let this heavy weight from the past pull you back or reduce your forward momentum.

FOCUS ON WHAT YOU DO NOW

At the risk of attracting criticism from a lot of other self-help authors, I want you to focus on the eternal present. If you think about it, all you have is the present. At any point in time as you read this book, you're always in the present.

This is one of the most powerful concepts you could never wrap your mind around. This is one of the most powerful ideas you could employ in your daily waking life. Why? The past already happened. Unless you have access to some sort of time machine, you're not going to make those facts go away. You can choose to interpret them in a different way. You are definitely more than welcome to change how you cope with them.

However, as far as the facts are concerned, they are set in stone. They're gone. That ship has sailed. By facts, I'm talking about who, what, where, when, how, and why. Bury the past. Let it go. Stop trying to change the material facts. It's not going to happen.

If you understand this, why are you beating yourself up about something that happened a long time ago? Why burn up all this emotional energy when you could have directed that power to get to where you need to go today? That's right, the eternal present.

Similarly, why are you worried about things that have yet to happen? Whether it's the next day or the day after that or a couple of months from now or even years from now, why are you worried about stuff that may not happen?

I hope you understand what's going on here. When you're torn between the past and the future, your emotional center is at risk. You have this center of emotional gravity and you're just wasting it, either pushing it forward to the future and worrying yourself sick or throwing it away by thinking about stuff from the past. You have to center your emotional ownership on action that you're taking now. This works on many levels.

RELENTLESS DETERMINATION

First, let's start with the obvious. When 100% of you is present now, you're more likely to make the right decisions. There's a higher likelihood that when you look at the big picture, you are able to make the right calls and the right outcomes will proceed from your actions. This leads to less regret and more happiness.

Second, when you center your emotional center of gravity to today, and I'm talking about right now, you are less likely to procrastinate. You are less likely to blame others for your failures and setbacks. There's also a lower likelihood that you will feel like some sort of victim and waste precious time feeling sorry for yourself.

Best of all, when you center your emotional focus to this very moment, you're able to look at the hard task right in front of you, and hit it again and again. These are the tasks you fear, so you come up with all sorts of excuses how you can kick the can down the road. You don't do that when you are 100% emotionally and intellectually here.

Finally, and this is extremely important, when you focus on the present moment, you show yourself that you're serious about pushing forward to your ultimate goal. Your audience is yourself.

If you do what a lot of other people to and dwell in the past and its guilt, regrets, anger, insecurity and whatnot, or you waste time worrying about stuff that has yet to happen, you are showing yourself that you're not serious. You're showing yourself that whatever it is that you are aiming for is really not all that important because this stuff from the past or the anxiety of the future takes priority. Do you see how this works? Do you see the mixed signals that you are sending yourself?

You have to understand that you are made of different layers. There is the conscious self and the subconscious self. You have to always be clear about the signals you're sending yourself because it's resonating to all of you, and if your conscious mind is conflicted, what you think your subconscious will do?

The message becomes loud and clear. You're not serious. Whatever it is you desire is really not all that desirable because look at you. You're torn in many different directions. You're going all over the place and emotionally you're chasing your tail.

So, don't be surprised if you find yourself in that frame of mind barely making progress towards your goal, and all of this can wear down your determination because it seems that as hard as you work and regardless of how many sacrifices you make, you can barely budge an inch.

Take Ownership of Your Ability to Choose Your Response

From this point, you have to be purposeful and conscious of how you respond to everything around you because you are constantly sending messages to your subconscious. For you to reach your life's great destinations and live up to your destiny, your subconscious and your conscious mind have to line up.

How do you make this happen? Take ownership of the fact that you are able to choose at any given moment. What choice are you making? You're choosing how to respond to the stimuli the world sends your way. Your mindset interprets the things that you see, hear, touch, taste, and smell. These produce thoughts. Thoughts are judgments. They are never neutral.

Once you start thinking and interpreting, you develop emotions. Again, thoughts are never neutral because they always trigger some sort of emotional state. Once you're in that emotional state, you take action. Maybe you say something to somebody or you do something.

Whatever the case may be, once you get to that stage, there are consequences. That's the point where you drop the pebble onto the surface of the pond. What happens next? That's right ripples. When those ripples hit an object, there's usually a reaction. What happens next? The world sends you even more stimuli.

Those words that you said out of anger, because you couldn't hold your tongue, you can bet that's going to trigger a different set of words from the person you spoke to or the person who heard what you said or the person whom you talked about. This then triggers more thoughts on your end, more emotions and actions, and on and on it goes. This is how you change your life.

You may be thinking to yourself, 'Wow! This is great. So, I'm moving forward.' No! This can work for people who are stuck and feeling frustrated as well as for people who are riding an upward spiral to a positive feedback loop to their ultimate goal.

Regardless, you can take control of this process. How? Focus on the weakest link. Here's a hint. It's not this stage where you're taking action. At that point, it's too late. In fact, too many people act on impulse. Sure, they can give you all sorts of rational-sounding explanations once you called them out on it, but when they make that first move, it's usually out of impulse because they're in a certain emotional state. They were triggered.

It's hard to control this chain reaction from the action stage. It's a little less difficult at the emotion stage but it's still going to take a lot of work. Instead, hit this process at its weakest link. This is the point where you develop thoughts. Change your mindset.

Do This Regardless

Regardless of the specific conditions you find yourself in, you have to make it a point to consciously and purposefully respond one way: to keep pushing forward to your goals. If this isn't part of the mix and if this isn't the highest priority item on your agenda, you're going to get stuck. What's the point of making great strides and then stopping for what seems like ages and then inching forward and then spurting forward again and then stopping?

Do yourself a big favor and constantly keep pushing forward. Whatever the trigger from the past may be and whatever the worry from the future looks like, keep pushing forward. This should always be your purposeful and conscious response. When

RELENTLESS DETERMINATION

you do so, you build determination on an almost unimaginable level because you become predictable in a good way.

WHAT ARE YOU WILLING TO SACRIFICE

I've heard it said that we all start out as potential, but somewhere along the line, we make decisions that hold that potential down or even stop it from manifesting into reality.

The storybook character of Peter Pan is a child in an adolescent form. Not any child, mind you, but a child who made the conscious decision of never growing up. So, he remains a potential trapped in that form.

We must stop to analyze why Peter Pan wanted to stay that way because Peter Pan, it turns out, was afraid of becoming Captain Hook. That's how he defined adults, so he'd rather stay a kid.

One of the things that you give up when you become an adult is you sacrifice a lot of those possibilities to map out a few paths ahead of you. Just as a child can theoretically become a millionaire, a lawyer, a doctor, or world leader; he can become a plumber, janitor, construction worker, farmer, or factory worker. As they select one option, the rest of the options close. This is called sacrifice.

All of us, as we grow, will have to make a decision as to what sacrifice to make. It's going to happen. If we don't make that decision, that sacrifice will be made for us. It is no surprise then that people who don't plan their careers end up doing work that they hate.

I wish I could tell you that this would fit common stereotypes of the frustrated doctor working in a factory. He could have been a doctor but now he works in a factory and he hates what he does for a living.

However, it could also actually be the opposite. There are a lot of kids in Middle America who decide to go into law or medicine because they think that's what their parents expect of them. Once they go through all those many years of education, they find themselves in careers that numb their soul. Sure, they're making a lot of money and they have a high social status, but they die each and every day because that's not what they want to do. It doesn't deliver the kind of happiness and fulfillment that they desire.

The reason too many of us find ourselves in this predicament is because we didn't consciously choose our sacrifice. We decided to hang on to this vague notion that all this potential is still open to us but, as we got older and older, the doors start too close and, before you know it, those sacrifices were made for you, and you find yourself in a life that you didn't choose.

We have to choose our own sacrifice. How do you do this? Be conscious that you are making that sacrifice. Becoming an adult means letting go of dreams and ideas because if you're in your 20's right now, you probably have millions of startup ideas going through your mind. As you play one video game after another, all sorts of game concepts go through your mind.

The problem is you're an adult. Pretty soon, you might have people depending on you and I'm talking about your kids and your significant other. What then?

One common example of this is when a young father lets go of his juvenile ambitions of becoming the next big time hip-hop star or video game designer to provide for his family by focusing on his career or business idea.

Be clear about your need to sacrifice. Once you're able to wrap your mind around the fact that sacrifice is required for you to live out your destiny, you then realize that life is a series of trade-offs. For one path to become activated, other paths have to die.

You cannot look at them wistfully and say I could have been or should have been or would have been. No, stop playing that game. You're wasting precious emotional resources when you do that. You have to completely turn your back on that. Sure, a wave of nostalgia might wash over you when you look at old photos of you freestyling at a hip-hop event, but you're a father now with kids about to go to college or you're a mother now providing for your family. You have to let go of what comes easy.

This where a lot of people who remain mental juveniles struggle. They say to themselves, 'Well, I want to be a video game designer' or 'I just want to be a singer.' Do you know how hard it is to be a successful game designer?

It's easy to become a failed game designer. In fact, it's too easy. You wake up one day, you're all pumped up about this hot idea for a game. It turns out that other people have hot ideas, and they end up in the same place as you. They're struggling. Very few make it to the top. By the top, I'm talking about making over a million dollars a year, much less hundreds of millions of dollars a year.

Most people in the video game industry are barely scraping by. If you don't believe me, go to the Steam platform and check out all the game titles in all the categories. They are too many. All those titles that you see represent dreams or 'hot ideas that can't fail.'

You have to sacrifice. I'm not saying that awesome idea for a video game is not going to be your destiny. However, if that is your destiny, then sacrifice everything else. This is where people drop the ball because in the back of their minds when they're playing Xbox games that they are somehow pursuing their dream of becoming a video game designer. No. That is not what is happening. You're just giving an excuse for your video game addiction but not really working towards your goal.

I hope you can see the difference. Be clear about your need to sacrifice and, just as importantly, go through with that sacrifice. When you make the sacrifice, you realize that your goal of becoming a video game designer has to be paid for painfully. There are things to learn and dues to pay.

Believe it or not becoming a video game developer is not as sexy as you may think. It's not all about ideas. You have to execute those ideas. Many of those ideas, believe it or not, are dead ends.

Your Determination Grows as You Make One Sacrifice after Another

Make no mistake making sacrifice is never easy. In fact, it can be painful. It's painful because you let go of pride. You also turn your back on things that used to define you. These things were pleasurable. You used to do these things all the time.

However, now that you have decided to become an adult, you're going to have to turn your back on those and put them away for good. When you're able to make one sacrifice, your ability to make another sacrifice increases and, before you know it, you scale up your sacrifice and, by logical extension, scale up your rewards.

Here is the good news. When you make sacrifices, there's always a reward because life is a series of trade-offs. Your determination grows when you're able to do this. It may be one of the most impossible things in the beginning but, as you get used to it, you notice that forward momentum. It becomes harder and harder to stop you at this point.

LET YOUR MEASUREMENT OF SUCCESS DRIVE YOU FORWARD

As the old saying goes, comparison is the thief of joy. How many times have you found yourself looking through your friends' Facebook timelines? Has the thought ever occurred to you that they're enjoying much better lives than you?

Have you gone through a celebrity's Instagram account and walked away with a distinct empty feeling? You're left wondering, "What did I do with my life? It seems that everybody's lives are so much better."

If any of this has happened to you, welcome to the club. You are hardly alone. In fact, every single day, millions upon millions of people go through the same exact ritual. Believe it or not, this is part of the reason why social media is so attractive and popular.

There's just something in us that makes us want to compare our lives with others. Maybe this has something to do with basic survival. Imagine you were walking through a forest, tens of thousands of years ago. You're with your buddy. Maybe you were foraging for food or water.

As you make it through the trees, you see a bear. You know full well that the distance between that animal and you and your friend is not large enough for both of you to survive. Both you and your friend start running.

At that point, there's only one thing that matters: who is faster? In other words, your ability to compete can save your life tens of thousands of years ago. Now imagine generation after generation of human beings passing this on through their genes.

We have a tendency to compare ourselves to others because we're competing and this competition is not pointless. It has been seared into our DNA because it meant the difference between life or death. It's either your friend gets eaten or you.

Guess what. It's very hard to turn that off. There's always this need to compare yourself to others or put yourself in some sort of hierarchy and figure out where you are in that pecking order or totem pole. If you work for a company, you look at yourself in the organization chart. How high are you up there?

If you go to school, you look at your class ranking. How close are you to #1 or where are you in your class percentage wise? Are you in the top 5 percent? When it comes to sexual attraction, you rate others on a scale of 1-5 or 1-10.

Don't be embarrassed. There's nothing to apologize for. This is all too human. Competition, ranking, and hierarchy are built into our DNA. It has to be, otherwise, we would not have survived. It's no wonder that people constantly compare themselves to others on social media.

What social media isn't showing you

Here's the rub. When you look at your friend's vacation pictures in Paris and check out the big smiles on his family's faces with the Eiffel tower behind them. You're not really looking at your friend and his family.

Instead, you are comparing your life with theirs. They seem to have it made. Obviously, they have the money to travel. Last I checked, it takes thousands of dollars to get on a plane to go on a 2-week vacation to Europe.

When you see these images, it's not about your friend. Instead, you start thinking about your life. It's not unusual to think that you have the short end of the stick. Here you are, toiling away at your cubicle or factory job and your buddy from junior high school is out there taking snapshots of himself and his hot girlfriend on a beach in Tahiti.

He's a professional blogger enjoying the very best that life has to offer jumping from continent to continent, enjoying all these amazing exotic foods and here you are, stuck at a dead-end job, unable to pay your rent.

Does any of this sound familiar? Does any of this cut close to home? Again, you are not alone. This is precisely the situation too many people find themselves in.

The reason why you feel miserable, frustrated, or, in any way, unhappy is because you are missing something that social media won't tell you. When you look at those pictures, you look at select snapshots of people's lives.

Do you think they'll show pictures of them struggling with the rent? Do you really think that they will show pictures of them getting in a fistfight with their significant other or getting thrown in jail for domestic abuse?

Do you really believe that people would show images of their expulsion letter from college because they cheated? How about videos of their boss reprimanding them because they screwed up on a project?

People won't post that kind of material and, for good reason, you probably wouldn't either nor do I recommend it. The problem is when people post their pictures and videos online, they post the highlights of their lives.

We're talking about marriages, baptisms, family vacations, global blogging adventures, you name it! These are the bright spots of one's life. Believe it or not, you have them too. But you also know that they are few and far between.

So you get this illusion on Facebook that this is what people's lives should be. But those are different people. If you are to look at what's usually going on in their lives, it's not much different from yours. They have struggles, bills to pay, things to worry about, health concerns, I can go on and on.

What's really going on here and what social media doesn't show you is that you are mentally comparing the low or mediocre points of your life and their high points. That doesn't make any sense.

That's like trying to compare 2 countries and for 1 country, you show its very best. I'm talking about skyscrapers, amazing airports, great public parks, and national monuments. And for the other country, you show slums, people dying on the street, homeless defecating in public areas. Is that fair?

For that second country, believe it or not, there are also skyscrapers and beautiful landscapes that people from all over the world would want to vacation at. But you don't see that.

In your comparison, you are lining up amazing skyscrapers that reach out all the way to the heavens made out of steel and glass compared to shanties comprised of rusting corrugated iron and half-naked children wallowing in squalor and poverty. Is that fair?

And guess what. It is you in the slums. That's your life. No wonder people feel miserable. It's not a surprise that they feel that the best things in life missed them. You can't help but feel inadequate when you do that.

But that's the subtle psychological reaction people have to Facebook, Twitter, Pinterest, and definitely Instagram. You look at the very best that people have and you compare it with your low and mediocre points.

You beat yourself up when you do this.

The bottom line: Your measurements determine your performance

What happens when you go through your social media feeds? You can't help but feel inadequate. You might even feel ugly or unattractive. Again, this is all-natural because you're looking at people at their very best and you're comparing yourself to them.

It doesn't occur to you to compare your very best to theirs. But, for whatever reason, you can't help but do this over and over again. It's as if you have an addiction. Deep down inside, you know that this doesn't make any sense.

But the emotional damage has been done. You feel small and insignificant. You feel poor or even a victim. And before you know it, it feeds into the narrative that you've been repeating to yourself again and again. Life is unfair and you're a victim.

Again, if this is your train of thought, you are not alone. A lot of people think this way. But what they don't see is that they can always choose to use a different metric. Who said you have to line up the slums of your life to the skyscrapers of your friend's life?

Nobody forced you to do that. You did that to yourself. Just as you can choose to do that, you can choose to do something else. This is why it's really important to measure your success in such a way that it helps you instead of hurting you.

You can't run a race thinking about how much faster everybody else is. That is your metric. If that's how you measure your success, you're making your job so much harder. It's going to emotionally and physically erode you. Your confidence is going to be shot and guess what, when the starting gun goes off, you're just not going to have it.

More likely than not, you're not going to give it your very best because at the back of your mind, at some point, you've already given up. Be very careful how you measure your success. Measure it in such a way that it drives you forward.

A lot of people, believe it or not, measure their success in such a way that it pulls them back. They think about their past failure and disappointments. They think about the times they were embarrassed, humiliated, or put upon. They can't help but think about the times when they felt that things were unfair or they were cheated. None of that is helping. None of that can help.

What you need to focus on is a way of measuring success that keeps pushing your forward and asking you for your very best step after step, inch after inch, day after day. What follows is a discussion.

In one way, you can measure success that will increase your determination. In fact, it will make you relentless.

You're only as good as your last success

For a lot of people, this is very hard to accept. For a lot of people, they feel that there has to be a better way forward because judging themselves based on their last success is too much of a tall order. Why? Most people are lazy. I hate to say it.

When you judge yourself by your last success, this automatically means that you had a last success and this requires work. How come? It's easy to look at the shallow reality of your life and say "I don't have any success. How can I judge myself by my last success when there is no success?"

Think about it. The fact that you have selected this goal instead of another lower standard or lower quality goals is a form of success. But it's not just the selection of that goal. Anybody can do that. No! The fact that you have decided to put one foot in front of the other and work towards that goal, that is success.

When you define yourself based on your last success, you build on what you've done. On day 1, you may have taken 10 steps to get to your goal. The problem is that goal is many miles away. No problem. On day 2, you take 20 steps.

So you're moving up. You went from 10 to 20 and then on day 3, maybe go for 50. That is your last success. You know you're not making the kind of progress you should be making when on day 4, you go back to 10 steps.

Do you see how this works? Don't think that just because you didn't zoom out of that starting gate like some sort of rocket that you've automatically failed. Don't do that to yourself. Don't cheat yourself.

Focus on your last success and say to yourself, "I'm only as good as my last success. I cannot coast. I cannot take a step back. I cannot relax and slack off. I got to keep moving forward." That's how you build determination.

You become hungrier and hungrier as the results come in and guess what. Something else is going on. You become more skilled. Your journey starts to change you. As you are able to connect the dots and become more efficient at what you do to achieve your ultimate goals, you become more competent.

Before you know it, you start developing momentum. Have you ever noticed that when you're doing any physical task, the first few times you did it was very hard? How can it not? You're still trying to learn the ropes.

But as you figure things out, it becomes easier and easier. Funny how that works, right? The truth is the more you do something, the better you get at it. This is why it's really important to understand that you're only as good as your last success. Meaning you have to keep building on that base and you have to keep improving on that base.

That's how you define success. As you go up and you start to scale and it becomes easier and easier. A lot of the emotional intimidation of the learning curve disappears. You start experimenting and before you know it, you become more efficient because it turns out that a lot of these experiments lead you to a faster, better, and cheaper way of doing things.

Whatever you do, don't lean on the past

RELENTLESS DETERMINATION

I know that the road ahead is hard. In many cases, the twists and turns and ups and downs make it very scary. Who wants to fail? Who wants to be disappointed? Who wants to be frustrated? Here's the problem. You have to push through. You have to do whatever it takes to keep pushing forward.

This is how you build determination every single day. It is the purposeful action of moving forward that helps build your determination and makes you relentless. Just how relentless do you need to be?

If you can't make it to the front door, try the side door. If that is a no go, try the back. If that is off-limits, try the basement. If you don't have any luck there, try the roof. If you can't make any progress today, try tomorrow and then the next day and the day after that.

Day after day, week after week, month after month, year after year. That is relentless determination. It doesn't happen overnight. You don't develop that level of dedication instantly. You build up to it step by step.

The worst thing that you can do is to turn around and say "I've gone this far. I deserve a break. I can coast. I owe it to myself." Get those ideas out of your head. Before you know it, you will fall into the trap of holding yourself to lower and lower metrics of success.

You reverse the progress that you have achieved up to this point. Previously, you were thinking along the lines of "I made it to 2 steps on day 1 and 4 steps on day 2. Surely I can make it to 6 steps of day 3." Do you see the pattern there?

If you are not careful, you can quickly reverse this. You can say to yourself "I've made 10,000 steps before. I owe it to myself to just do 2 steps today and take it easy. I earned this reward." Guess what happens the next day. It becomes just as tempting to say "I want to slack off as well. As long as I'm putting in 2 or 3 steps, I'm fine."

RELENTLESS DETERMINATION

What had been an amazing journey at a decent clip has stalled. Don't fool yourself into thinking otherwise. That's really what happens. You hit a wall. But this wall is not physical. It's all in your head.

The worst part is you think you deserve it. The right measurement of success. What is the right measurement of success required to build relentless determination? The best analogy I can come up with is a car jack. If you've ever had to replace a flat tire, you would know how a car jack works.

You pump the jack and it would go up. You pump it again and it would go up. It never goes down unless you turn it to release the pressure. In other words, when you ratchet up your efforts, your proper measurement of success enables you to stay at that level until you ratchet it up again and again.

The wrong measurement of success enables you to go back down. You're never back down when you're using the right measurement of success to build up your determination. Now you may be thinking that this is great to hear and it's definitely easy to say. But you know full well that it's hard to do.

But here's the good news. The more you do it and the more you confront the difficulties on the road ahead, it becomes easier. Eventually, momentum will catch up to you. As I have said earlier, the more you do things, the better you get at them.

This is not magic. It's not like something that just occurs to you. As you do it and you devote the proper amount of attention to detail to your task, you start to connect the dots. You start to figure things out. You get a big picture view and everything starts to fall into place and guess what happens.

You're able to make the necessary connections adjustment and things that used to take forever, you're able to do in a shorter period of time. Similarly, things that were so difficult on a mental level, now they become second nature to you. It's as if you know them like the back of your hands.

How come? Not only does intellectual familiarity lead to better solutions and efficiency, there's less emotional intimidation. This is not your first time to the dance. You know where everything is, you know how things work, generally speaking. You know what you can play around with that would lead to the results that you want. The ease scales up without you necessarily sacrificing your standards.

Ground your measurement for success in actual results

You have to ask yourself "Am I producing excellent work?" You can't lie to yourself. You know full well what excellent is and what mediocrity looks like. Don't play any games. This is very hard to do because our natural tendency is to coast.

"Why should I put in the work when I can get a decent result putting in less work?" This is how the human mind normally works. Minimum input, maximum output. Well, if you believe in excellence, you believe in putting in your best and expecting the best.

"Good enough" is never ever good enough. You have to ask yourself "Is this excellent? Is this the best? Does this leave everybody else in the dust? If not, why not?" This is a hard question to ask because what you're really asking of yourself is to oust your natural tendency to coast or to produce "good enough" work.

In other words, it's a revolt against your all too natural human tendency for mediocrity. Believe me, this is an almost irresistible temptation. Why? As you work your way towards success, maybe you're an associate at a law firm and you know full well that you're going to have to put in hundreds of hours at the office to move up.

It's tempting to just do the bare minimum because you know that the road ahead of you is so far away. The reward that you crave seems almost unattainable. Are you really going to beat yourself up when you know full well that even if you do your best, you're just inching forward to the success that you desire?

In many cases, it doesn't even feel like you're moving forward inches. It often feels like you are stuck in place. In that context, does it make sense, on an emotional level, to do your best? This is what you have to override. You have to overcome this.

Regardless of who's looking and regardless of whether you get fancy medals or awards or stickies or whatnot, you're still going to do your best. You're still going to leave everybody in the dust. Are you willing to do that? Can you make the sacrifice?

This is the price you pay to be the best. It has nothing to do with whether people will pay you what you're worth or if you will get the proper recognition. You're not doing it for that. You're doing it to build determination because once you are able to establish relentless determination, nobody can stop you.

Nobody in front of you and inside you. I'm talking about self-sabotage. This is why you have to believe that the only measurement of success is that you are only as good as your last success and you better build on that success.

That is what pushes you to be your very best. This is the light that you need to shine on what constitutes excellent work. Otherwise, you're just going to be playing semantic games with yourself. You'll find yourself in the position of "This is excellent enough because it's better than anybody else here. So why should I try even more?"

If you're the best in your office pool, why not be the best on your floor? Once you attain that, why not be the best in the building? Once you reach that, why not be the best in your industry? Do you get where I'm going with this? Good.

That's the level you should operate at. At that point, you're unstoppable. People cannot intimidate you because your results precede you. People can talk a good game, they may have a lot of connections, but your results scream for you. You cannot be denied.

You have to understand why you need to be the best. Don't think of it as just some lofty idea. That would be nice if that happened, but not really all that practical. Get that out of your head.

Understand why you need to be the best

Being the best must exist on its own. It cannot be tied to money or any other kind of reward like a claim, external validation, industry recognition, sexual magnetism and attraction, and other rewards. All of these are great things. You can't use them as replacements for your direct goals.

Instead, you have to be the best because it's internally driven. When you're looking for sexual attraction, validation, a claim, recognition, status, and money, you're looking for other people to reward you.

As I've repeatedly pointed out in this book, you can't control other people. You know it. You're at their mercy at that point. A lot of them will find a lot of reasons not to reward you but then, what do you do in that situation? You are at their mercy.

On the other hand, when you are aiming for the best and that is your metric of success, it is internally set. Only you know when you have delivered the best because you cannot lie to yourself if you focus enough.

When you decide to be the best, you are driven by a fire that burns from within. It cannot be taken away from you and it cannot be denied by other people.

Best of all, no one can control it. Only you. So, why be the best? You should pursue it because it is a reflection of your chosen values.

RELENTLESS DETERMINATION

People chose to be mediocre. Everybody else around you chose to do the very minimum to get the most rewards but that's them. You've selected a higher standard. You chose to be the best and this means that excellence is a reflection of your character.

You have to understand that when you are living for other people's approval, what you're really doing is wanting to develop the right reputation. Again, there is nothing necessarily wrong with that but the problem is you want to have control because reputation really boils down to what one person saw and chose to say about you.

Another person who hasn't really seen you work or hasn't really seen you in certain circumstances would then repeat what that first-person saw who may not have seen all of you or have seen you in many different contexts. That person repeats that information and another person repeats it because that first person is quite influential and before you know it, you have a reputation but does your reputation actually mirror who you really are? Of course not.

How can it be? How can it? Reputation is really all about what people say about you. They don't know you deep down inside.

On the other hand, your character is who you really are because if you have a certain character, you would think, act, and feel a certain way regardless of whether people are looking at you, and regardless of whether you are in public or not. This is who you are even behind closed doors.

When you choose to be the best, and you desire excellence in everything you do, it is a reflection of your character. You have made excellence. A touchstone of your character.

And guess what? It is unstoppable because no matter how many people lie about you, and no matter how you're misunderstood. If you truly are the best, your works will scream out your character.

They can curse you to your face, hound you, and even chase you out of town. But, if you truly are a good person, your goodness will precede you.

On the other hand, if you're a scumbag, you know how that works. Be the best, choose excellence it's never a waste of time.

CALL THE SHOTS

I can't believe that there are too many people out there who think their choices do not have consequences. They think to themselves, "when I said something at a certain time to somebody, what's the big deal?"

They might wonder what an action (that they thought was so small and inconsequential) was met with such a backlash. Make no mistake. The world often doesn't see you the way you see yourself.

Too many of us think that we're just another face in the crowd. We're convinced that no matter how hard we try and what kind of plans we have; our actions are not going to have much of an effect.

Too many of us have given up. We have assumed that we were born, we grow up, we get sick and then we die. When we look back at the lives we lived, there's not much of a trace.

It's kind of like walking along the beach and stopping to turn to see what happened to your footsteps. They got swallowed by the tides. It's as if you were not there.

This is how a lot of people think. Not surprisingly, it is reflected in their lives. They just do the bare minimum to get by. They don't want to be excellent.

They don't want to produce the best. They don't want to deliver the highest value. They don't want to be bothered with any of that. They just want to get by day to day, paycheck to paycheck.

You have to understand that if you're in that situation, nobody is forcing you to live like that. It may seem like you're forced by circumstances. Look at the force behind those circumstances.

The answer might shock you. If you're like most people, it might upset you. The truth is we live the lives we deserve. I know that's a controversial statement. I am sure that is not politically correct.

Too many of us spend our time looking for someone or something to blame for how our lives turned out. Let's be honest. This is wasted energy.

It is because while you chose the life that you are currently living, none of this means that you can't choose another life. I want you to wrap your mind around that.

It's easy to see the negative aspect of that. It jumps out at you. You can't help but feel guilty and angry. There's something else going on. Focus on the ability to choose.

Just as you can choose your life right here right now, you could have chosen another life. Instead of regret, I want you to do something different. I want you to look at the future. Focus on the big goal that you have.

Say to yourself, I choose that life. What I'm saying is that you need to call that shot. Just because you have given up the responsibility or abdicated your control over this whole process doesn't mean that it doesn't exist.

Let me break it down further. Your life (I'm talking about everything that other people can perceive about you) is the effect, your thoughts are the costs.

Instead of recoiling in horror and claiming victimhood, which is all too natural for so many people, look at this for what it is. This is amazing news. It's good news.

It's as if freedom was proclaimed to prisoners in their cells. It's as if you've spent all this time feeling walled in by this mental prison. Only to wake up one day and realize that the key has been in your palms all along.

You need to take that key. Put it in the lock and turn it. That's how you will open all the doors in your life. These doors lead to new possibilities and opportunities.

How does this all work?

Our lives are caught in a call and response dynamic with the world. We are not in an echo chamber where we say, I want this and then it bounces back to you. It doesn't work that way.

Instead, the world is always looking to react to what you do, and to a limited degree, what you say. Action triggers a reaction. Does that sound familiar? It should.

It's true for physics. It's also true for metaphysics, psychology, sociology, and everything else. You are the author of your life based on what you do. So write a new chapter, write a new book, edit the characters, flip the script.

Again, this is a fact that doesn't sit well with a lot of people. The logical implication is if you are in any way unhappy with your life, then where does the blame come in?

It's not with your parents. It's not with the third-grade bully that gave you wedgies. It's not school administrators, your boss, your first girlfriend or boyfriend, your first husband or wife. None of those people are to blame.

People don't want to pick up that responsibility. You don't want to step up to that. None of that denial is going to make this fact go away. You took an action and the world reacted. Repeat this many times over and you have your life.

The bottom line is your actions have consequences. It had consequences in the past. This is playing out now. Guess what? This is going to continue along in the future.

The world is simple

As complicated as your day to day world may be and as confusing, frustrating many of its details may appear to you, the world is quite simple. It is objective. If you do something, there will be consequences.

At work, if you do something positive like you produce a lot of work and it has the highest quality work, it's going to have consequences. Just because you don't see the immediate consequences of your actions doesn't mean that nothing is happening.

It's like watching an ice cube melt. The moment you take that cube from its tray in the freezer and put it out in the sun, something's happening. It may look like it's taking forever because the puddle doesn't instantly appear.

However, if you give it enough time, that ice cube that seems to refuse to melt the first few minutes eventually leaves a puddle of water. The same applies to your actions.

You just have to keep it up. The more you focus on this, the more your determination grows because you know that you have this iron law of the universe working for you.

The moment you become conscious of this is the moment you're presented with a golden opportunity to make it work for you. The reason why so many people are frustrated is that they are unconscious about this process.

They think they can just live their lives and not have to worry about the consequences. They take one action after another. They end up in a certain life. Guess what?

It's all too predictable because these are consequences of earlier actions. Nothing happens in a vacuum. Your life is not an accident whether you like it or not. The world is objective.

It doesn't care about your motivations and intentions. It doesn't play this game of " would have, could have or should have". All it cares about can be boiled down to one simple question: what did you do?

The Solution

With all the above said, the solution to your struggles as you chase after your destiny is to be clear about the actions you send out to the world. That's all you need to do. Be clear about your choice of actions.

When you do this, you understand that some actions trigger a certain range of consequences. Other actions attract another range of consequences. These are not neutral.

Some are very negative. Others deliver mediocre results, and others can produce very positive outcomes. Be clear about the actions that you send out and increase your control over the consequences.

Oftentimes, you don't get the exact consequence that you desire. Welcome to the club! Most people don't have that 100% control. You'll never get that control.

By being as clear as possible about your actions, you increase the chances that you will get the consequence that you had in mind. This is how you shape your reality.

Let this personal power of choice over your actions push forward. This should make you more determined. Once you start seeing that you can produce certain results, you quickly wake up to just how much power you have over your life.

Your life no longer has to be the product or the consequence of what mistakes your parents made. You no longer have to be a slave to the past.

Instead, by focusing on the eternal present and your ability to choose today, this very moment, you shape your reality. You get closer and closer to the destiny you chose. So choose wisely, be intentional.

That is power. That is the internal engine that produces very real results. That can't help but feed the fires of your determination.

This is how you remain motivated because, at the bottom of it all, you can always come back to the central fact that you can choose your thoughts. If you can do that, you can choose your actions.

Your actions can then trigger a certain range of consequences. This is how you produce and shape your reality. You're no longer this piece of plastic on the surface of storm-tossed seeds just being pushed by the winds from one end to the next.

You're no longer living in a world you didn't create among people with their selfish agendas. It seemed so hostile. You felt so lost. None of that is happening because now you can focus on the power you have.

Nobody can take that power away from you. Even if they were to physically put you in prison, you can choose to respond differently. This response doesn't just stay in your mind.

It is manifested in the words that you choose, the emotions that you feel, and most importantly the actions you take. Those actions have consequences.

The more intentional you are, the more control you have

As I keep repeating in this book over and over again, so many of us allow our past (with its trauma and drama) to define us. Stop it. You don't have to let that rob you of the actual control you have over your reality.

Instead, allow yourself to be motivated by the clarity of the vision you have set up for yourself. It doesn't matter how poor your parents were when you were born. It doesn't matter how little love you received when you were growing up.

RELENTLESS DETERMINATION

It doesn't matter how many heartaches you went through, and betrayal and backstabbing you suffered. It doesn't matter how much abuse you suffered, nor does it matter if you abused other people, committed crimes, betrayed others. Let go of that crap.

That's the past. You take control of today. Stop beating yourself up over past bad decisions whether you committed a crime, had an abortion, did all sorts of drugs, went to jail, failed classes, never graduated. I can go on and on.

Let those remain in the past. You're here now. Even if all that stuff just happened yesterday, you're here now. Allow yourself to feel in control because you can choose your actions today.

Maybe in the past, it felt like you're just throwing spaghetti in the wall. You were just hoping that somehow someway, something will stick, and your life will turn for the better. This used to be my approach but now I'm much wiser.

Those days are over. Now, you are going to be intentional. You understand that the values you have chosen for yourself lead to certain mindsets that enable you to interpret reality in a certain way.

Your thoughts change. Your words have become transformed. Your actions take a different path.
Once everything reaches the level of action, all bets are off.

That past pattern of negativity, defeat, failure, mediocrity, embarrassment, pain, and frustration? That's the past. Be intentional in everything that you think, say, and do.

You will be able to call the shots as far as your day to day reality is concerned. It doesn't matter whether your boss gives you the reward that you crave.

It doesn't matter if people pat you on the back and say you're doing an amazing job or you're a good person. They can still do what they're doing. They can still ignore you. They can still talk behind your back.

People might even shun you because they think you're a criminal or you did something that they don't approve of, but it wouldn't matter. You know that you are headed somewhere else; to your destination and path.

You know that you are better than the present circumstances that you find yourself in. You know that you are producing the best and you have one clear North star, which is excellence.

All that negativity, crab mentality, and backstabbing are not going to transform you into a person you don't want to become, or worse yet, pull you back where you started.

None of that has to happen. You have to give yourself permission to choose and take ownership of your actions today. The more intentional you are, the clearer the outcome becomes.

The more you work towards that outcome (I'm talking about the day to day results that you produce), the more things scale up. As I mentioned repeatedly, the more you do something, the better you get at it.

When you keep this up, you reach the point of mastery. You know it like the back of your hand. Isn't that awesome? Wouldn't it be great when you reach a point where you can call the shots?

I've got some good news for you. All competent and successful people start as rookies and apprentices. They had to be led around by the hand.

Still, since they were so focused on where they wanted to go, and the kind of people they want to transform themselves into, they allow the self-reinforcing process that I've described above to push them to greater and greater levels of mastery. Take the late, great Kobe Bryant for example. He came out of high school into a game with grown men, yet had the mind set and mentality to master his craft and dominate. He leveled up to arguably the best player who ever played the game.

You can do it too. It's never too late. I don't care if you just got out of school or you're 16 years old or you dropped out or you're in your 80s. As long as you're drawing breath, there is still hope. You can still allow yourself to master anything.

Keep at this call and response process

This is where your determination is tested. Do you think it's easy to just wake up one day and say, I'm going to take ownership of my life, I'm going to be as intentional about my goals, and I will act accordingly? I wish it were that easy.

I wish it was just a simple case of some magic statement that you read to yourself, somehow someway your life is magically transformed overnight. It doesn't work that way. That's a fantasy. That's the stuff of Hollywood movies; that's fantasy.

We're talking real life here. In the real world, you're going to get a lot of pushback. In many cases, a lot of this bad reaction is going to come from you. You're going to hold yourself back. You'll get kicked in the mud and left to die.

Part of your mind (whether you're aware of it or not, and whether it's expressing these terms or not) will say, who do you think you are? You're a failure. That's all you're capable of.

You came from a family of failures and mediocre people. Do you want to be the best? Give me a break. You haven't done anything excellent in your life. Now, you expect things to turn around today. Who are you kidding?

I'm sure you can come up with your list of statements. All of us do it to ourselves, even the most successful people. There will always be a part of us that's not going to be with the program. Why? We're creatures of habit.

Whether you like it or not, part of you enjoys the

frustration and misery that you feel. How come? They're not obligated to change. Somebody may be in a miserable marriage or relationship. They would stay in that relationship.

Even though they know it doesn't feel good, they could do so much better, it's killing them deep down inside, but at least they know what they're dealing with. Their fear is so great that they'd rather stay where they are.

I want you to be completely honest with yourself and acknowledge this part of you. It's nothing to be embarrassed about. All of us have this shadow.

Until and unless you realize that you have the shadow, it's very easy for you to fall for its whispers. Why? This part of you is not going to talk to you when you are pumped up and you're just doing your best.

It's not going to appear when you are enjoying forward momentum. It seems that every action you take to get closer and closer to your ultimate goals is bearing fruit. You're well within this positive feedback loop.

Things are panning out. No. That voice will appear when it seems that you put in all this time, you sacrificed so much, and you don't get the results that you feel you deserve. Resist the enemy of doubt, kill him.

You push forward and then you meet somebody that is just a stone wall. This person has made it his or her job to make you miserable and nothing else.

That voice also appears when it seems like you're making so much progress and then all of a sudden, a black swan appears. It could be a virus, stock markets tanking, industries collapsing, war, you name it.

Be ready for that course because nobody, and I mean nobody on this planet can hold you back and push you down worse than yourself. When you do it to yourself, it seems so natural.

It might even seem like this is your destiny. This is who you are. If that isn't daunting enough, there are other things outside of your control like disasters, resets, misunderstandings, push backs, you name it.

You have to keep pushing forward and understand that you are sending out this signal to the world through your actions. This is a call and response process. God created you for greatness and it's your job to fulfill it.

The more intentional you are in the signal that you send out, the more predictable and effective the response will be. Before you know it, you'll get to where you need to go. However, along the way, you're going to have to take your lumps and bruises.

Success isn't about getting knocked down for a loop. Successful people have been beaten down. Not just once, not just twice but many, many times. What makes you so special? You expect to get knocked down but you get back up.

The good news is success is not about getting knocked down or even knocked out. Instead, it's all about how quickly you get back up, and how focused you are in calling the shots again and again until you get the response you intended.

This is how you build determination because you commit to getting back up. You commit to the fact that there will be mistakes and setbacks down the road but you're ready for that. You know that you're better than that conclusion.

This book has all the information that you need to go from someone who constantly asks, "What happened? It's not fair" to someone who makes things happen. I'm not just talking about a person who just gets things done.

I'm talking about a person who plans and makes that plan come to life. Wouldn't it be awesome to turn the ideas that flash into your mind into something that you can see hear, touch, taste, smell, feel and enjoy?

Wouldn't it be great to have this rush of positive emotions and pumped up feelings that you have regarding your plans to translate into reality? You have all the information to make that happen.

Most importantly, you have all the information you need to keep going. Once you decide on your ultimate goal, you can create the self-reinforcing process that you need to constantly find that determination required to make that plan a reality.

Relentless determination means the ability to keep going forward regardless of what happens around you and what happens to the road in front of you. It means not having to be dependent on external circumstances.

It means that regardless of how challenging it may be, you will eventually find yourself at your destination. It is a character trait. It is not something that happens to you overnight nor is it some heirloom that your parents drop at your lap.

It is something that you have to develop. I wish it was some sort of one-time big-time kind of thing. No. You have to build it day by day, one painful inch after another.

The good news is the more you stick to something and the more you work on your determination, the easier it becomes. Your character changes each step of the way. Before you know it, the journey has transformed you into a different person. The person that you desired to be.

I wish you nothing but the greatest success, serenity, peace, joy, and love.

ABOUT THE AUTHOR

Andre Thornton is a poet, writer and author who continues to inspire readers with his deep sense of spirituality and realistic points of view. He has been writing for over 20 years and continues to pursue his quest for self-improvement while helping others reach their potential. Andre has an M.H.A degree from Louisiana State University-Shreveport and currently works as a Program Analyst for the U.S. Government. His previous titles include: Mental Conceptions: A Poet's Dream, Awake Even in Sleep, Still Dreaming, and Poetik Alchemy.

CONNECT WITH ANDRE
Via
Email: andrerthornton@gmail.com
Instagram: andrethornton_the_author

www.ingramcontent.com/pod-product-compliance
Lightning Source LLC
LaVergne TN
LVHW051604080426
835510LV00020B/3127